Dump Your Phone, Find Your Person

A Research-Based Guide
for Dating in the Modern World

Anne Marie Bessacini

Printed in the United States of America

Bessacini, Anne Marie.
 Dump Your Phone, Find Your Person
 ISBN: 978-0-578-55210-1

First Edition: August 2019

THX

Endless thanks to my sister and parents who have always wholeheartedly supported every weird endeavor of mine, and who have always gently nudged me toward becoming a writer.

Thank you to the friends, family, and strangers who cumulatively spent countless hours discussing and contemplating this book with me. There would be nothing to fill these pages without your help, so for that, I thank you.

Lastly, thank you to The Hive in Santa Monica whose matcha lattes and avocado toast powered 90% of the writing of this book.

Contents

Preface

Background Stuff

Don't panic. "Dump Your Phone" does *not* mean what you think it means. At no point in this book will I tell you to ditch your smartphone or abandon all the conveniences of modern technology. That would be insane. This book is about dating in the modern world, and we will occasionally talk about how your smartphone can sometimes impede you from meeting *Your Person*, whether that be your future husband, wife, partner, boyfriend, girlfriend, or soulmate. So now that you've hopefully breathed a sigh of relief and released the death grip on your phone, let's talk about what this book *will* be about.

This whole "writing a book" thing started after a chat with my dad, who calls every so often to offer me unsolicited dating advice. "I just have no idea where to find single people in real life" was the sentence that kicked off this particular chat; however, this conversation wasn't anything out of the ordinary. I'd found myself talking about dating more and more often recently, searching for answers to the infinite questions I had about being single. In a world ruled by technology, it was starting to feel like the only way to meet someone was through a dating app, and I wasn't crazy about that idea. I am a market researcher by day, so I half-jokingly told my dad that I was going to conduct some research to figure out where to find single people in real life.

So I did. I wrote a survey about dating and sent it to all my friends— and begged them to send it to their friends, coworkers, family members, etc. It gained momentum, and soon I had three times as many responses as I had hoped for. My initial motivation in doing this research was admittedly selfish: I wanted to understand the habits of single people and where to find them so that I could apply the findings to my own dating life. However, after pouring through the data, reading through countless messages I received, and talking more in depth to friends, family, and strangers about the findings from the research, I realized that keeping this data to myself just didn't feel right. All single people needed to hear this.

More important was the fact that all my single friends *wanted* to hear about the research findings. Shortly after taking the survey, many of my single friends, coworkers, and acquaintances sent me messages. They wanted to know when I would have the results, and if I could share them. Some people told me about realizations they had while taking the survey. Some people were vulnerable and shared their dating successes and failures with me. It was fascinating, and I felt privileged to be the gatekeeper of their data and their stories. It felt like the survey had sparked conversation and introspection among the single people who had taken it. There was a renewed energy and honesty in talking about dating, a kind of comradery perpetuated by the survey. Perhaps for the first time, people started to realize that they were not alone in how they felt about dating.

Because of all the interest in the survey, I decided to create a quick, five-page PDF that I could send to my single friends. It was going to have a few cute infographics and lessons learned from the research I conducted. That "five-page PDF" slowly morphed into the book that you are reading right now. The data from this research was just so vast and fascinating that it warranted a much more comprehensive analysis than I originally intended.

Unfortunately, the original survey was done with what we in market research call a "convenience sample," which basically means that I sent the survey to a group of people who were easy to reach. You can imagine that my group of West Coast dwelling, twenty-something-year-old friends were not exactly representative of all single people in the United States. At this point, I realized I needed to do this research the right way. I paid a third party to run the same survey among a demographically representative group of people so that the results would accurately depict the population of the United States. While the data from the original survey was certainly interesting and educational, the second round of data (which is the data depicted in this book) is infinitely more powerful because it offers a more accurate, holistic view of the single people across the United States.

Research is empowering (especially when it's done in a legitimate, controlled way), and I want you to feel empowered by the findings in this book. While countless books on dating have been written based on opinion or personal experience, this book is based on real-world data from hundreds of single folks like yourself. I want that real-world data to instill a sense of confidence in you. I want it to motivate you to dump your phone and find Your Person.

Most importantly, I want the data in this book to give you a sense of comfort in knowing that you are not alone. There are legitimate reasons why it feels so difficult to date in today's world, and I hope this research will prove to you just how normal your feelings about dating are. If you're single, use the data in this book to your advantage and reference it if you start to feel a little lost in today's complicated dating world. Use it to take the first steps (however small) to improve your dating life. If you aren't single, use this data to encourage and motivate your single friends. Regardless of your relationship status, use this research as a catalyst for conversation, reflection, and change.

Be forewarned that this book is truly the blind leading the blind. I am not an expert on love, and I don't have a PhD in the psychology of dating. I'm a single girl in Los Angeles who realized that there are profound issues in the modern world of dating and realized that I want to be a part of trying to solve those issues. If this book can help just one single person feel more confident about navigating the dating process, I'll have considered it a wild success. I don't want this book to come across as being rooted in dating expertise, but I do want it to come across as being rooted in research. Just remember to take everything you read with a grain of salt, knowing that your beliefs and experiences may differ from the data depicted here. So without further ado, let's dive in.

Preface

Nerd Stuff

If you're a data nerd like me, or if you care about the methodology behind the research in this book, read this page. If you couldn't care less about where the data came from, go ahead and skip this page and jump straight into the good stuff.

All of the data that appears in this book came from a quantitative survey conducted in June 2019. 605 people aged 21-44 completed this online survey. 409 of them were single and 196 were in a relationship. Quotas ensured that survey completions among 21-44-year-olds were representative of census demographics in the United States along the lines of age, gender, and region. Below are the demographics of survey participants.

Gender & Sexual Orientation	Total	Ethnicity	Total
NET: Females	51%	White or Caucasian	61%
Female, heterosexual	43%	African American	18%
Female, bisexual	5%	Hispanic or Latino	11%
Female, asexual	2%	Asian or Pacific Islander	7%
Female, homosexual	1%	Other	3%
NET: Males	49%	**Cityscape**	**Total**
Male, heterosexual	43%	Urban	31%
Male, bisexual	2%	Suburban	46%
Male, asexual	<1%	Rural	23%
Male, homosexual	4%	**Region**	**Total**
Age	**Total**	West	22%
21-24	24%	South	36%
25-34	54%	Midwest	23%
35-44	22%	Northeast	19%

1

Why Is This So Freaking Hard?

Here's the thing: sometimes being single sucks. Even the most optimistic among us can sometimes feel like dating in today's world should be considered cruel and unusual punishment. What did we do to deserve this misery? Obviously, not everyone feels this way; some people might love the dating process and all that comes with it. This book probably isn't for them. This book is for the single people like me who feel that they could use a little help.

The world of dating has changed rapidly with the rise of technology, and people everywhere are doing their best to understand it. Dating apps have caused a major disruption, and single people everywhere are still adjusting to this new tech-driven reality. Dating is a topic that interests everyone—from renowned psychologists with doctorate degrees, to Aziz Ansari, to Instagram influencers. There are countless books, podcasts, documentaries, movies, and TV shows that attempt to highlight the shifts and changes we are currently experiencing in both the technological and dating world. There are infinite online dating boards filled with people lamenting their dating lives and seeking answers from complete strangers on the internet.

It's for good reason that dating is such a hot topic right now. Dating is crucial to finding a serious relationship, which many of us desire for our futures. It's a prime time to be doing research on dating because there is still so much frustration associated with the modern dating process, all of which has been exacerbated by our dependence on technology. 48% of single people surveyed agreed that they feel a little hopeless about their dating life. While a little depressing, there's also something comforting about this fact. When it comes to dating, half of your single friends are struggling to feel optimistic about it—regardless of whether they admit to it.

In fact, at the end of the survey, there was an open-ended question that asked people if they realized anything about themselves while taking the survey. Many people said that they realized for the first time that they may not be alone in feeling a little down about dating. And how right they were! We'll see throughout this book just how universal the feelings about dating are.

Now, let's clear something up before going any further. Feeling a bit down about dating in no way means that all single people are miserable. Single people lead fulfilling, amazing lives and many are completely secure with who they are, what they've accomplished, and where their life is taking them. But to be more specific, it's the *process* of becoming "un-single"—if you will—that we don't necessarily enjoy. Becoming un-single is often both emotionally and physically exhausting. If there is one way to sum up the data from the research, it's that dating and trying to find that special someone appears to have taken a toll on a lot of us single folks. It takes a certain stamina to go through the process of becoming un-single.

In summarizing the woes of single people in this research, it would appear that there is an overall air of confusion and frustration regarding the dating process. We'll talk about a variety of issues that contribute to these feelings throughout the book.

Some of the core issues we will address are:
- Technology has dealt a serious blow to our dating lives, whether we realize it or not. The opportunities to meet

other people in real life have dwindled and our dependence on smartphones for everyday tasks is at an all-time high.

- We don't know where to find other quality single people in real life. We may or may not be intentionally trying to seek them out, but we seem to be stumped about where to find them. We may also not be trying as hard to find people because we have the security blanket of things like Netflix and Hulu waiting for us at home. Why go through the discomfort of trying to meet people in real life when we could just rewatch *The Office* for the seventeenth time?

- Even when we are in a place where single people might be, we don't know how to go about approaching them because we are absolutely terrified of making the first move, and our smartphones often put up a barrier to meeting new people in these situations.

- A lot of us are riddled with social anxiety, insecurities, or fear of being rejected—all of which can keep us from putting ourselves out there and approaching people we're interested in. We default to using our phones when these negative feelings arise instead of facing them head-on.

- We feel that no one is approaching us or showing interest in us, and we might internalize or blame ourselves for this. In reality, technology is largely to blame for the lack of human interaction and connection in real life.

- We are frustrated by the amount of effort involved in using dating apps; we swipe endlessly and start conversations that often end in disappointment.

There are a lot of ways to look at the data collected in this survey. You could draw some pretty morbid conclusions about the modern dating world, but that's not how we're going to look at it in this book. We're choosing to look at the data as a crucial set of information that we need to start improving our dating lives. We're choosing to look at it as something that unites us single people and offers us the rare insight into how other single people are really feeling (not what they are projecting on their social media accounts).

If you're anything like me, you probably have friends and family alike offering unsolicited (or solicited) dating advice. How many times have you heard this from the various people in your life? *"Put yourself out there!" "Get off the couch!" "Mr. Right is just around the corner!" "There are plenty of fish in the sea!"* Nothing makes a single person shut down faster than hearing cliché advice that is seemingly not rooted in any truth.

However, sometimes we *do* all need a little tough love—a little kick in the pants to remind us that we have the power to take our dating lives into our own hands. Throughout each chapter, I'll include some brief advice denoted as *Tough Love.* It's called *Tough Love* for two reasons. First, because it won't necessarily be easy for you. It's challenging to get out of your comfort zone and break out of old habits or old ways of thinking. Second, it will be the blunt advice that you need to hear—even if sometimes you don't want to hear it. The difference between this *Tough Love* and your parents' tough love is that mine is rooted in *cold hard facts.* The *Tough Love* I'm giving you isn't coming from the bottom of my heart; it's coming from the quantitative analysis of the research compiled from hundreds of single people across the United States. Hopefully, that will give you more confidence and motivation to implement some of this advice in your own dating life.

Think of these *Tough Love* tidbits as your cheat-sheet for dating—the SparkNotes of the book. Instead of re-reading the entire book when you lose sight of your dating goals, skim through and look for one piece of *Tough Love* that you can start implementing immediately. Baby steps are better than no steps at all. When you fall back into feeling a little lost or forget the changes you want to implement, refer back to these *Tough Love* tidbits. Dogear your physical book or add a bookmark on your e-book—whatever you need to do so that you can reference them quickly and easily.

Tough Love

There's no need to rush through this book and attempt to implement every change at the same time. It's not realistic or sustainable, and would probably be quite frustrating. Focus on one chapter for a couple of days, a week, or even a month. Take the time to reflect on the *Tough Love* sections throughout the chapter. You can choose to either dig in your heels and refuse to give this *Tough Love* a chance, or you can choose to get out of your comfort zone and take a small step toward improving your dating life. Let's do this together!

2

There's No Way People
Are Enjoying This... Right?

So, how do single people feel about the dating process? Sometimes, we swap hilarious stories of dates gone wrong, or team up to overanalyze the texts from our crush, but we don't often have deep conversations with our single friends about how the dating process is impacting us physically or emotionally. In fact, only 28% of single people say they talk openly with people about how their dating successes and failures make them feel. To solve this mystery, let's take a look at one of the very first questions in the survey: "How much do you enjoy the dating process?"

How much do you enjoy the dating process?

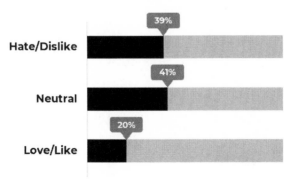

Indeed, 39% of single people report *hating* or *disliking* the dating process, with another 41% of people feeling *neutral* toward it. That leaves just one out of five single people who report *liking* or *loving* the dating process. In an interesting twist, almost half of single women report *hating* or *disliking* the dating process, compared to less than a third of single men. There are a few other demographic groups of people who are significantly more likely to report *hating* or *disliking* the dating process: those aged 35+, LGBTQ folks, and those who live in rural or suburban areas.

There's also an interesting correlation between enjoying the dating process and overall life satisfaction. 51% of single people say they are *very or somewhat satisfied* with their life overall. Compare this to people in relationships, 64% of whom say the same thing. So overall, single people are slightly less likely to report high life satisfaction than people in relationships. This is important to recognize because life satisfaction appears to impact many facets of dating, almost like a domino effect. 29% of single people report *low* overall life satisfaction, and 51% report *high* overall life satisfaction.

According to the data, single people who report high overall life satisfaction:
- Go on more dates
- Enjoy the dating process more
- Are more satisfied with their dating lives
- Feel more hopeful about their dating lives
- Are more confident in their appearance
- Are more likely to make the first move
- Feel more optimistic that they will meet someone great
- Are more likely to be on the lookout for single people

I want to point out one thing here. The way the data is described above (as well as some of the other data throughout the book) highlights data that is *correlative* in nature, not *causal*. It's not necessarily that something like 'high life satisfaction' *causes* you to go on more dates, but the two things may have a high *corre-lation*. It's not a definitive equation that you can use to say, "If I increase my life satisfaction, then I will start going on more dates." It's a bit more nuanced than that, so keep an eye out for these types of *correlative* relationships in the data throughout the book.

Because of the correlation of high life satisfaction with these other positive behaviors and attutides, it is important as a single person that you prioritize your overall life satisfaction. Not only will it help you be more successful in the dating world, but it will also bring you more happiness overall. It's easy to fall into the belief that you might find happiness when you meet the right person; however, it's important to take your happiness and life satisfaction into your own hands instead of relying on someone else for those things.

I'm not saying that you need to put your dating life on hold until you have achieved complete nirvana. Enjoying your life as a single person and also desiring a relationship are not mutually exclusive. You can do both. You can find ways to bring more happiness into your life while also going on dates and looking for a partner. I personally enjoy the fact that I currently have endless time to pursue my hobbies and interests, but I'm also hopeful that my future holds more time spent with a significant other. The bottom line is this: if you are unsatisfied with your life overall, it's unlikely that going on dates will bring you the happiness you crave.

Tough Love

Be honest with yourself. Are you doing everything in your power to improve your overall life satisfaction? Are you doing things that bring you joy? Are you taking the risks that you always wanted to take? Enjoying your life while single is a huge predictor of how successful you will be in finding a healthy, happy relationship. Being happy with yourself and your life should be prerequisites before entering into any long-term relationship. Do some brainstorming on your own to think about things you could be doing to bring more joy and satisfaction into your life.

Let's get back to how people feel about the dating process. Only 20% of single people say they enjoy the dating process. This just reiterates the idea that you might enjoy your life as a single person without really liking the dating process. After all, single people are most likely to choose the words *free* and *optimistic* to describe how they feel about being single. They're much less likely to choose "negative" words like *disappointed, sad*, or *frustrated*. So, even when your dating life isn't so hot, most single people still feel a sense of freedom that can trump a lot of the more negative feelings about the dating process. I mean, think about being single for a minute. You can do whatever you want to do and go wherever you want to go. You don't have to choose which family to visit over the holidays, and you get to choose how to spend or save your money. There's no one to judge you if you want to eat mac and cheese for breakfast or watch *Parks and Rec* all day with no pants on. There's also no one to distract you from finally taking a risk you've always wanted to take. The freedom that comes with being single can be invigorating.

Our friends in relationships may even occasionally wish they were single—certainly not because they want to go through the painful process of dating, but because they miss the freedom and flexibility that comes with being single. So, while we're on the topic of what's great about being single, let's look at some of the reasons that single people might like the dating process.

WHAT WE LIKE ABOUT THE DATING PROCESS

While only 20% of single people report *liking* or *loving* the dating process, the majority of single people can come up with at least a few things they like about it. There's something for everyone: from meeting new people, to getting your dinner paid for, to hooking up with someone new. Here are the top reasons people enjoy the dating process. *Note: Some verbatim comments from anonymous survey takers have been included throughout the book.*

1. It can be exciting and fun to meet new people.

According to the survey, 52% of single people say that meeting new and interesting people is something they like about the dating process. The dating process can be fun for those who genuinely like meeting new people, making conversation, and are otherwise at ease with some of the awkwardness inherit to the whole process. As an added bonus, the more people you meet, the closer you get to finding Your Person, which is why 39% of single people say that "getting closer to meeting their significant other" is something they like about the dating process. If you ever become frustrated with dating, it's good to come back to this and reframe your mentality. At the very least, you are meeting new people and getting closer to finding Your Person.

"It's fun meeting a lot of new people and the anticipation of what you might find makes it exciting."
– Female, 21-24

2. Dating gets you out of your bubble and encourages you to do things you haven't done before.

Dating is a great way to expand your horizons, which is why 44% of single people say that "doing new things or seeing new places" is a reason they enjoy dating. With this knowledge, we can take some baby steps toward improving our dating lives. If we know that single people are interested in doing new things and seeing new places, we can prioritize this when planning a date. If you only go on (or plan) dinner-and-drinks dates, it's easy to become disenchanted with the process. Try to inject some fun into your dating life. Suggest a creative first date that gets you both out of your comfort zones. Not only will this make for a more memorable date, but it also might ease the dissatisfaction that can come with dating. If you can reframe your mentality about dating as a way to be exposed to new people and places (as opposed to a means to an end), it might take away from the pressure of finding your soulmate.

"I find it exciting because dating shows me all sorts of people and all sorts of possibilities, and making connections with new people is great."
– Male, 25-34

3. If we're being honest, sometimes it's just nice to get attention.

The third most common reason (41%) why single people like the dating process is because it makes them feel desirable or attractive. We're human, and it typically feels good when someone expresses interest in us. It can be an ego boost to get some much-needed attention. 32% of single people say they like the feeling of being pursued by people who are interested in them, and 18% say they like the ego boost they get from dating. It makes sense that dating is an effective way to fulfill the human need for attention.

"I like someone giving me their undivided attention and making me feel as though they enjoy my company." *– Female, 35-44*

4. You'll usually learn more about yourself in the process of dating.

Of the single people surveyed, 38% said they view the dating process as an opportunity to grow as a person and get out of their comfort zone. Another 34% say they like learning more about what they want in a partner. While dating, it's easy to place focus on the other person, but it's actually a great opportunity to be introspective and learn more about ourselves. With each date, you can refine the list of what exactly you want in a partner. That's not to encourage you to make a super stringent list of requirements that no one will ever live up to, but it may help to prioritize the important things. For example, maybe you've always thought a sense of humor was a non-negotiable. But the more dates you go on, the more you realize that humor isn't as important to you as something like honesty or compassion. Use dating in this way to learn more about yourself and what you want in a partner.

"I love getting to know different personalities. It helps me to discover hidden things about myself and what I expect in a relationship."
– Female, 35-44

---

5. We all need some lovin' (physical or emotional).

One of the top reasons for enjoying the dating process, according to 32% of the single people surveyed, is the "physical or emotional affection" that comes with it. As dates progress, getting closer to someone emotionally is a rewarding experience. The butterflies and warm feelings you get when someone starts caring about you are one of the best parts of dating. Many people cite the physical closeness as an added benefit, as well. When it comes to hooking up with people, 29% of men say this is a top reason they like dating, while only 9% of women say the same thing. Compared to their respective counterparts, hooking up is

DUMP YOUR PHONE, FIND YOUR PERSON

much less important for women, people looking for a serious relationship, and those age 35+. Single people who enjoy using
dating apps are also much more likely to cite hooking up as a
reason for liking the dating process when compared to those
who don't like using dating apps (43% vs. 17%).

*"The sex is what gives me the motivation to get
close to someone I like."* – Male, 25-34

6. Being wined and dined by a date is a nice perk.

Having meals and drinks paid for is much more likely to be cited
by women as a reason for liking the dating process (23% of
women vs. 9% of men). For some women, going on dates is a
legitimate way for them to cut down on their grocery bill. However, for other women, being wined and dined is actually more
symbolic of something greater. Some women view having their
dinner paid for as an indicator of their dates' generosity, security, confidence, or seriousness about a relationship.

*"I like the idea of having someone take me out for
a good time, particularly if they agree to pay for
the meal. I like the idea that someone might be
willing to take care of me."* – Female, 25-34

That wraps up the major reasons why single people like the dating process. If we're willing to open up our eyes, there are
actually a lot of positive aspects of dating. There were certainly
a few single people who said they didn't like anything about the
dating process, and that's fair. It's easy to get down on dating,
especially if you haven't felt successful in dating recently. However, it's good to keep this list of positive things in mind and use

them to reframe our mentality if we start getting too negative, which we'll talk about next.

Tough Love
Try to find at least one reason why you might enjoy the dating process, even if it's as simple as, "I like getting out of the house" or, "It will be nice to eat dinner with someone." Being able to find the positive things about dating will help you when some of the more negative things inevitably happen.

If you found it hard to relate to any of the reasons to like the dating process, maybe the next section will be more your speed.

WHAT WE <u>DISLIKE</u> ABOUT THE DATING PROCESS
On the other hand, the things that people dislike about the dating process could probably fill its own book. There are movies, TV shows, books, podcasts, comedians, etc. that feature the dating process, and there's a good reason for that. It's ripe with scenarios that are awkward, hilarious, or painful, and they all make for great entertainment.

While looking at the data for why single people dislike the dating process, it became clear that the things we *dislike* overwhelmingly outweigh the things that we *like*. This section will highlight some of the most common complaints about dating with one goal for doing so: to reiterate that we are all going through the same thing. I'm sure at least one, if not all, of these reasons for disliking the dating process will resonate with you. This might be a lot of negativity to throw at you so early in the book, but we need to set the stage before we go about trying to fix these issues.

1. Putting yourself out there is scary AF.

A whopping 49% of single people agree that the fear of being rejected is one of the worst parts about dating. Being vulnerable and putting yourself out there can be terrifying when you don't know whether the other person feels the same way about you. This fear of rejection can be completely crippling and can get in the way of talking to and meeting new people. Rejection sucks—there's no way around that—but in subsequent chapters, we will talk about how to change your mindset so the potential of rejection doesn't have as much power over you.

"I think it's just hard to step out of the comfort zone and take a risk on someone you really like."
– Male, 25-34

2. Honesty and respect have taken a back seat.

The lack of honest, transparent communication—and the lack of respect for one another's feelings—make the entire dating process more painful and awkward than it should be. The lack of transparent communication, according to 39% of single people, is one of the reasons they dislike the dating process.

"Essentially I hate playing 'The Game' aspect of it. I'd prefer if the person was straight forward."
– Male, 25-34

3. Being "in my feelings" is nowhere near as fun as dancing to the Drake song.

The negative feelings that arise during dating can really nudge us toward disliking it all together. The most commonly mentioned feelings that make people dislike dating are feeling nervous and anxious before a date (39%), feeling insecure about whether people will like you (37%), feeling disappointed after a date (33%), and feeling uncertain about when you will meet a significant other (28%). Insecurity and uncertainty are common among both men and women, but the feelings of nervousness, anxiety, and disappointment are more prevalent among women. They're also more common among people who say they dislike the dating process, meaning that people who enjoy the dating process are less likely to struggle with these negative feelings. It's actually quite natural to want to avoid the dating process if it causes unwanted negative feelings.

"I don't like dealing with the anxiety and pressure of meeting someone new. I'm scared of rejection."
– Female, 25-34

4. Ghosting and flaking is a real confidence-killer.
Ghosting, flaking, and fizzling conversations have all become increasingly common with the rise of dating apps, and 36% of single people cite this as a reason for disliking the dating process. We have dating apps to thank for the rise of socially-acceptable ghosting, and we have society to thank for perpetuating this habit outside of dating apps. It's a bummer to actually be ghosted by someone you're interested in, and it's also a bummer to be constantly wondering if you are *about* to be ghosted. If this happens enough times, it can seriously degrade your sense of self-confidence. We'll talk more about ghosting later.

"I don't like how people can be disrespectful and prefer to ghost you instead of being upfront and saying they no longer want to see you."
– Female, 21-24

5. It can be discouraging when other people's relationship goals don't align with your own.

One reason why single people say they dislike dating, according to 34% of those asked, is because there are too many people who aren't serious about wanting a relationship. It's notoriously difficult to discern who is only interested in a casual hookup and who is looking for a more serious relationship. This is more likely to be cited as a dislike among women (41% vs. 26% of men) and women are also more likely than men to say that they are frustrated with the lack of high quality single people that they meet (42% vs. 24%). Lastly, a lot of women go on dates in hopes of meeting someone and getting to know them, but many feel that there are expectations of being physical too early in the dating process. Of the women asked, 44% say they dislike the expectation of sex or physicality during the dating process (compared to only 17% of men who say they dislike this).

"Many guys talk about wanting something serious, but they just want sex." – *Female, 25-34*

6. Dating can feel like a competitive job interview.

Dating can feel much like a job interview where you feel the need to always be "on" for your dates. According to the survey, 28% of single people say that trying to make the best possible impression is something they dislike about dating. It's hard to relax and be yourself when you are trying to blow someone away on the first date. And similar to a job interview—where you're trying to figure out if you and the interviewer are jiving— 28% of single people also dislike the part of a date when you are trying to guess what the other person is thinking about you. Trying to make a good impression, feeling like you have to rise to the top of candidates, and trying to guess what the other person is thinking are all things that can contribute to an exhausting dating process.

"It's pretty nerve-wracking meeting all of these new people and trying to make a good first impression." – Male, 21-24

7. The first date small talk stops being fun after the third time.

It might be exciting to tell a date about yourself the first few times, but continuously asking and answering the same first-date type of questions gets old quickly. 33% of single people agree that the repetitive first date conversations are a reason to dislike dating. For the folks who are more introverted, meeting new people and making small talk can be especially difficult and even painful. Introverts need more time to recharge after social interactions, and the dating process could take more of a toll on them than it would on extroverts.

"Talking about yourself and going through the 'getting to know you phase' can be tedious when you have to keep doing it over and over with new people." – Female, 25-34

8. Dating can suck up your time, energy, and money.

The entire process of dating can be mentally, emotionally, and physically draining—from trying to plan an interesting date, to trying to decode cryptic text messages after a date, to paying your credit card bill after a month of actively dating. It takes a toll on us simply because we have to pour so much time and energy into it. When it comes to reasons to dislike dating, single people list how physically/emotionally exhausting it is (32%), how volatile emotions are while dating (31%), how expensive it is (26%), how time consuming it is (24%), and how difficult it is to plan dates (22%). Women are more likely to find the process to be emotionally draining, while men are more likely to find it expensive. When we invest a lot of time, energy, and money into dating, it's easy to feel like the amount of effort you are putting in isn't exactly providing the desired "return on investment" when things don't work out.

"Repeating the same process of putting effort into someone and getting your hopes up for nothing is really exhausting and can be demotivating."
– Male, 21-24

9. Meeting single people IRL is difficult and/or extremely rare.
Seriously, *where* are the single people!? As it turns out, I'm not the only one struggling with the question of where to meet single people in real life. A quarter (25%) of single people say that trying to figure out where to meet other single people is a reason they dislike dating. As a result, many single people turn to dating apps as a solution, which we'll talk more about in subsequent chapters.

"It is difficult to meet people in a large city, especially when you don't know anyone or where to go looking for nice single people." – Female, 21-24

10. Datings apps have changed the game.
Dating apps have fundamentally altered the landscape of modern dating, and 24% of single people say they dislike dating for this exact reason. The survey data on apps is clear—single people don't really like them. They are shallow and frustrating for many people who wish there were better alternative ways to

meet people. Connections don't feel deep, and apps have made people feel disposable. We'll dive much deeper into dating apps later in the book.

"I really hate the apps, but it's so rare that people you meet in your actual life will ask you out. I don't like the app-based reality we live in."
– Female, 21-24

Phew. Are you still with me? That was a whole lot of negativity about dating. Taking a deeper look at why people dislike the dating process serves one key purpose: I want you to realize that you are not alone in how you're feeling about dating. Most single people dislike at least some aspects of dating. We shouldn't use this list of dislikes as justification to march onward hating the dating process. Despite having to deal with the more frustrating aspects of dating or not feeling successful in the past, it's important to remain optimistic about your future.

Here's just one important reason to adopt a more optimistic outlook on your dating life: Those who say they *like or love* the dating process are *three times* more likely to go on one or more dates in a month compared to those who *hate or dislike* the dating process (76% vs. 25%). In fact, how much you enjoy dating correlates to a ton of metrics.

Compare these subgroups of people who say they <u>like or love</u> the dating process:
- 8% of people who go on 0 dates
- 35% of people who go on 1+ dates
- 46% of people who go on 3+ dates
- 11% of people who rate their attractiveness as a 6 or lower
- 30% of people who rate their attractiveness as a 7 or higher

- 20% of people looking for a serious relationship
- 33% of people looking for a casual relationship
- 18% of people who have been single for longer than a year
- 33% of people who have been single for less than a year
- 41% of people who enjoy using dating apps
- 10% of people who dislike using dating apps

Keep in mind that the relationship between enjoying the dating process and the metrics shown above are *correlative,* not *causal.* So we don't necessarily know if people enjoy dating because they go on more dates, or if they go on more dates because they enjoy dating. Figuring this out can feel a bit like the question, "Did the chicken or the egg come first?"

Regardless of the answer to that question, it seems to me that if you are more cynical about the dating process, you might be putting yourself at a serious disadvantage. Several things could be happening if you are someone who dislikes or hates dating: you could be putting out negative vibes, which isn't attracting people to you; you might not be putting your best foot forward because you are apathetic to dating; you might be self-sabotaging any opportunities you have because, deep down, you believe that they won't work out; you might not be as likely to approach people; the list goes on and on.

The bottom line is this: Being cynical about the dating process isn't going to get us anywhere. There are many comparisons I could draw that illustrate how a cynical perspective puts us at a disadvantage. For example, you could watch the news every evening and hear about all the devastating events happening in the world. You could fall into depression and believe that the world is doomed. But the only person who is suffering in that scenario is *you.* The alternative option is to watch the news, acknowledge that bad things happen, but still believe that the world is fundamentally good. You can resolve to do your part in making the world a better place.

Dating is no different. You have two options. You can choose to dwell on the negative, but if you do this, you'll likely give up on meeting new single people or going on dates. But again, *you* are the only one who is suffering in that scenario. The better option is to acknowledge that there are aspects of the dating process that aren't great, but remain optimistic. It's up to you to find a way to make the dating process work for you. It's much easier said than done, but it's the option that will afford you the most success in the dating world.

Tough Love

Remember that your feelings about dating are entirely normal. Acknowledge that the dating process isn't always rainbows and butterflies. Things don't always go the way you want them to, and you're allowed to feel sad, frustrated, and lonely throughout the process. What you shouldn't do is allow those things to stop you from putting yourself out there. Get back on the proverbial horse, give yourself a pep talk, reframe some negative attitudes—whatever you need to do to pull yourself out of that funk. The more optimistic you are about dating, the more likely you will be to attract the type of person you are interested in.

3

What Does My Phone Have To Do With This?

We've established that dating is tough. There are plenty of things that make the dating process difficult, but one of them goes largely unnoticed: the rise of technology over the past decade. Subtle and not-so-subtle shifts have occurred as a result of our technologically-advanced world. These shifts play a huge role in why it feels so difficult to find and meet single people in real life.

Let's use our imaginations for a moment to picture what life would be like if we were thrown into the dating world during our parents' generation, a time when cell phone and internet technology were virtually nonexistent. What I want you to picture is life without all the modern conveniences of today's world—no Netflix, Amazon, Postmates, Instacart, Fandango, OpenTable, Instagram, Uber, Venmo; indeed, *no smartphones at all.* Imagine how differently you would spend your time if you didn't have access to all of these apps at your fingertips.

My most accurate guess is that our lives would have looked a *lot* different than they do now. We might be going to the local movie theater or Blockbuster store to rent a movie instead of watching Netflix at home; going to Target or CVS to buy household necessities instead of ordering them on Amazon; going to the post office to mail a letter instead of sending an email; visiting with friends and family instead of scrolling through their Instagram feeds; waiting in line at the bank to deposit paychecks instead of using a bank's mobile deposit app. You get the point.

Are you seeing a pattern here? What I'm trying to emphasize is the fact that, in general, we spend significantly less time than our predecessors did *out in the world*. The modern world is so hyper-focused on convenience and efficiency that there is increasingly less motivation to leave the house. Groceries, dinner, banking, entertainment, exercising, and even potential dates are all at your fingertips. That means that both you and your potential soulmate have exponentially fewer opportunities to meet each other out in the wild, simply because we are not out in the wild as much as our parents' generation and the generations before them.

From our modern-day perspective, we could say that our parents' generation "wasted" immense amounts of time because of the inefficiencies of the past. They spent countless hours doing things that we would absolutely not have the patience for nowadays. They lined up for hours outside of a movie theater to buy tickets for a premiere, waited for the Pac-Man machine to free up at their local arcade, drove to a restaurant to order takeout and waited for the food to be ready, and the list goes on and on.

Despite the inefficiencies of the past, the time our parents spent out in the world afforded them significantly more opportunities to meet and interact with other people. It was common to meet your significant other while filling out a deposit slip at the bank, and that's just one example of a place that has been rendered completely obsolete by technology. Long gone are the days when you would strike up a conversation with someone filling out a deposit slip at the bank. I mean, when was the last time you were even in a bank? And what is a deposit slip?

In addition to simply not leaving the house as often as our parents did, most of us have little to no tolerance for inefficiencies when we *do* leave the house. If you're anything like me, you might have made reservations for dinner on OpenTable, bought your movie tickets in advance on Fandango, ordered coffee to go through the Starbucks app, filled prescriptions at CVS via text message, made appointments via online portals, etc. So even when we *do* happen to leave the house, we tend to poise ourselves for maximum efficiency and minimal interaction with other humans. We utilize technology in order to avoid interaction with other humans, which has detrimental repercussions on our happiness, well-being, and our ability to meet our potential future partner.

Tough Love

Become more aware of all the ways you use technology in your life, and identify any possible opportunities that you may be missing out on because of your reliance on technology. Ordering your groceries online? Try popping into a grocery store in a trendy neighborhood instead. Ordering your Starbucks via mobile app? Try waiting in line and making small talk with the person in front of you.

I'm not telling you to waste endless amounts of time doing things that are completely inconvenient. I'm just telling you to be more aware of how technology has enabled you to be hyper-efficient when you are out in the world. Consider indulging in some of these inefficiencies here or there if it means you might meet someone new. Your goal of being out in public should not be to get in and out of every establishment in record time.

A more obvious fact is that previous generations didn't have smartphones to hide behind when they were out in public. Our generation notoriously uses smartphones as a crutch to avoid interactions we might find awkward or uncomfortable. In fact, 62% of people say they use their phones to cope with situations that are boring, lonely, or awkward. If you need an example of this, take a look around the next time you get in an elevator or are in line somewhere. How many people are scrolling mindlessly through their phones? Are you one of them? There are usually two types of scrollers: 1) the type who is engrossed in their phone and is completely oblivious to the people around them, or 2) the type who is actually hyper-aware of the people around them and is desperately trying to look busy on their phone so they don't have to engage in conversation.

This kind of mindless scrolling is just one manifestation of tech addiction. The whole call-to-action of this book is to "dump your phone" to open us up to the possibility of finding our potential future partner. But dumping our phones can feel really hard and even scary. According to the survey, 87% of people spend two or more hours on their phone each day. It's uncomfortable to think about what we could be doing with that time if we weren't on our phones.

Without seeming too dramatic, it's important for us to pause here to acknowledge the correlation between the increasing usage of technology and the increasing rate of mental health issues around the world. There are plenty of studies that link social media, smartphone, and tech usage to a whole host of mental health issues, such as depression, anxiety, and loneliness. The group that uses their phones to cope with situations that are lonely, boring, or awkward are significantly more likely to say they struggle with anxiety, fear of rejection, and low self-esteem compared to the group of people who don't use their phones as a coping mechanism. Spending too much time on our phones is wreaking havoc on our mental well-being, yet our phones are the first thing we reach for when we want to feel secure and safe. It's important for us to acknowledge the fact that the world of technology may not be all roses and rainbows; acknowledging this will shed some light on how technology impacts our dating lives.

Becoming aware of your dependence on your smartphone is crucial to understanding why it feels difficult to meet single people. How many times have we missed an opportunity to meet our potential soulmate because we had our noses buried in our phones? Our dependence on these devices has seriously hindered our ability to meet new people out in the wild. Our parents' generation would have been forced to make conversation with strangers if they were bored out in public. But our generation has our entire network of family and friends sitting in the palm of our hands, so why would we go through the discomfort of striking up a conversation with a total stranger? When the opportunity does come along for us to engage with a stranger, a good amount of people will avoid that interaction in favor of using their phone.

My goal here is to simply help you build your awareness. Maybe the next time you're out in public, you'll see who's mindlessly scrolling. You'll see someone pull out their phone and pretend to look busy the moment they step into an elevator. The allure of scrolling through your phone in public will hopefully start to fade when you realize that it's a mechanism that promotes social anxiety and loneliness. Once you start noticing these people out in public, my hope is that you won't want to be lumped in with them. Dumping your phone will feel much more empowering and appealing than burying your nose in it.

Tough Love

When you're out in public, put away your phone. I know it's hard to hear, but this is a change that is absolutely essential to meeting someone in real life. Have you ever had the realization that you're swiping away on dating apps, only to look up and see an incredibly attractive person standing in front of you? We are so wrapped up in our phones that we've all but put a sign on our forehead that says, "Don't talk to me." By putting away your phone, you are at least signaling that you are open to conversation.

Don't get me wrong: This isn't a miracle cure. People won't start flocking to you because you're not holding a smartphone, but we do need to become less reliant on our phones as a safety blanket. Be aware of how uncomfortable it makes you to put your phone away in these kinds of situations. At first, it will probably feel awkward to be the only person not on your phone. But it's okay, don't panic. Just feel the discomfort and anxiety—no matter how big they feel, know that these feelings will not kill you, and they will pass. Be curious about how often you use your phone as a safety blanket, and challenge yourself to get out of your comfort zone.

The more often you opt for human interaction instead of smartphone scrolling, the more comfortable you will become with being out in the world, making eye contact, smiling, and starting conversations. Who knows, you might even meet your future partner the way generations before us have—in real life.

We are moving toward a world where it's possible to exist with minimal to no human interaction. I know it sounds dramatic, but that's intentional. It's happening slowly and without many of us even catching on. Peloton sells an at-home stationary bike that connects you with a digital instructor—so you don't *actually* have to go to spin class. Amazon Fresh touts the convenience and immediacy of its on-demand grocery delivery service—so you don't *actually* have to go to the grocery store. Netflix is investing billions of dollars into creating movie and TV content— so you don't *actually* have to go to the movies. I could go on and

on because there are examples everywhere. We are slowly eliminating the need to leave the house, meaning that our
opportunities to interact with others are dissipating more and
more with each passing day.

How often do we stop to think about what we are sacrific-
ing as we gain increasingly efficient technology? We are much
more isolated than our parents were because we can opt to do
everything from home. Because we don't leave the house as often, because of our extremely low tolerance for inefficiency, and
because of our dependence on our smartphones, there are
simply fewer opportunities to meet and talk to new people in
everyday life than there have ever been before.

We are so conditioned to expect efficiency in every aspect
of our lives that our disdain for the dating process could also be
due to our perceived inefficiencies of modern dating. One common complaint is how "time-consuming" the dating process is,
but perhaps technology has redefined our standard for what is
"time-consuming." Our threshold is drastically lower than those
who came before us. If we are expecting to meet our soulmate
with the same efficiency as our Postmates dinner delivery
(which sometimes still tests our already-low patience threshold), we are bound to be disappointed and frustrated. So is it
actually the dating process that we dislike? Or is it just our disdain for having to put in the time and effort that we aren't
accustomed to?

These days, asking us to leave the house or deal with a
slight inconvenience is enough to make us throw our hands up
in frustration. When it comes to dating, we need to acknowledge
that technology has conditioned us to expect our tasks to be
easy. We also need to own up to the fact that leaving the house
and coping with inefficiencies are two things that our generation is not very good at, and those same two things are essential
in our quest to meet someone in real life.

I want to paint a picture of this technologically-advanced
world because I want you to understand that it's not *you*. It's not
your imagination telling you that it feels harder to meet single

people; it *is* harder to meet people. Generations of the past have had significantly more opportunities to meet and interact with people simply because they couldn't do much of anything from the comfort of their own home. They were forced to leave the house, or they would never get groceries, hang out with friends, or exercise.

Technology is a subtle hindrance in the world of modern dating, but we tend to overlook its role because of all its positive effects. It's a good exercise for us to bring awareness to this fact and make changes in our lives where possible. Thus far, we've only talked about technology in general—we haven't even touched on dating apps: That is a whole different beast altogether.

4

What's Going On Out There?

Technology has also increased our tendency to compare our-selves to others. This temptation is hard to resist when we are constantly bombarded with pictures on social media of our friends traveling to exotic places, influencers showcasing their extravagant lifestyles, or millennial millionaires starting their own companies. We compare our everyday lives to the highlight reel of the people we follow on Instagram.

We should obviously stop comparing ourselves to others for an abundance of reasons, but it makes sense why we might be doing it. There's always a nagging thought in the back of my mind that all my single friends are out on dates on Friday night while I binge watch *The Good Place* at my apartment.

The truth is that we really have no idea what other people's lives are like, and that's what makes the comparison game so dangerous. We have no idea if the extravagant influencers feel loved and supported by their friends and family, and we don't know if the happy couple with beaming smiles on Instagram is, in fact, cheating on each other. And we *definitely* have no idea if the people going on incessant dates from their dating apps are happy. Most of the time, we don't have the slightest idea of what other single people's dating lives actually look like.

The goal of this chapter is to shed a little light on your fel-low single people and what's happening out in the dating world.

Hopefully, this will give you some insight into what others are doing so you don't feel the need to compare yourself to them.

HOW MANY DATES ARE SINGLE PEOPLE GOING ON?

A whopping 66% of the single people surveyed assume that "other people go on way more dates than I do." Most of those people are assuming incorrectly.

How many dates do you go on in a typical month?

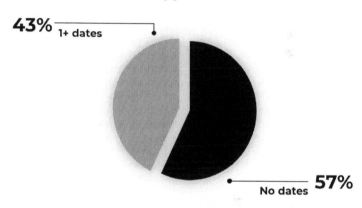

43% 1+ dates

57% No dates

The truth is that only 43% of single people report going on one or more dates in a typical month, and only 14% go on three or more dates. That's only four out of ten single people who have been on a date in the past month! Hopefully, that makes you feel a little more normal and a little less alone. When it feels like the whole world is going on dates without you, look at this pie chart and don't beat yourself up if you haven't been on a date in a while. If 43% seems low to you, remember that this number includes a wide variety of single people—people who are constantly working long hours, people who just got out of a relationship, people who are a little more anti-social, people who may feel more cynical about the dating process, etc. Regardless, you should know that even going on one date a month is not what the majority of single people are doing , and going on three or more dates a month is very, very far from the norm.

A few groups of people are more likely to be going on one or more dates in a typical month: men are slightly more likely than women (46% vs. 40%), those under age 35 are more likely than those who are 35+ (48% vs. 28%), and straight folks are more likely than LGBTQ folks (45% vs. 33%).

Tough Love
Try not to compare yourself to other single people or assume that everyone else is going on more dates than you. That's not the case, and it will only cause you to feel bad about yourself. If you feel discouraged, look at the data and remind yourself that it's normal not to be going on dates—57% of single people don't go on a single date in a typical month. We obviously don't want it to stay this way; the whole goal of this book is to get your confidence up and get you back out there. But for now, take comfort in the fact that most of us are not cranking out dates every month.

WHAT TYPES OF RELATIONSHIPS ARE SINGLE PEOPLE LOOKING FOR?
In the dislikes about dating, we heard from single people about how difficult it is to discern what types of relationships people are looking for. Sometimes, it can feel like everyone is looking for a no-strings-attached hookup. In reality, only 18% of single people say that they are looking for a "casual relationship with no commitments." The vast majoriy of single people are either looking for a serious, long-term relationship (40%) or are open to any type of relationship (42%).

Interestingly, the type of relationship you are looking for might be correlated with how much you enjoy the dating process. Among the people looking for a serious relationship, 44% say they *hate or dislike* the dating process. Compare this to single folks with different relationship goals: only 32% of people who are open to any kind of relationship *hate or dislike* the dating process, and only 23% of people who are looking for a casual relationship *hate or dislike* the dating process. Check out some additional stats below on people looking for a serious relationship and how this might be impacting their experience with the dating process.

Among people looking for a serious relationship:
- 65% wish they could skip the entire dating process and just be in a relationship (vs. 43% of casual-relationship-seekers)
- They are almost twice as likely to say "I feel a little hopeless about my dating life" compared to casual-relationship seekers (62% vs. 34%)
- 47% cite "feeling insecure about whether people will like me" as a top dislike (vs. 26% of casual-relationship-seekers)
- They are more likely to feel pressure about making a good impression compared to casual relationship-seekers
- They are twice as likely as casual relationship-seekers to use words such as *disappointed, sad, frustrated,* and *impatient* to describe their feelings about being single

These correlations suggest that the harder you are looking for a serious relationship, the less likely you are to enjoy the dating process. Why is this? It's possible that people who are looking for a serious relationship may be putting more pressure on themselves to find their soulmate, which can make everything much more stressful and frustrating. When you're looking for your soulmate, you are putting unnecessary pressure on both yourself and your date, which can make you more critical of both parties. You may be more disappointed when a date doesn't live up to your high expectations, or you might feel more insecure when someone doesn't reciprocate interest in you. The research suggests that dating may be more enjoyable if you aren't putting all that pressure on yourself to find your soulmate. That's not to say that you need to set aside your goal of having a serious relationship, but it might be worth it to keep an open mind.

Tough Love

Consider reframing the way you think about the dating process. While it's true that you may desire a serious relationship, approaching every date or interaction with this goal might be setting yourself up for failure and/or disappointment. If you can approach dating with a more lighthearted and open-minded mindset, you might find the process to be more enjoyable.

HOW LONG HAVE YOU BEEN SINGLE?

The amount of time you've been single can also make a difference in how your dating life looks. Can you think of a friend who has become recently single, say within the last six months? My guess is that, after the proper period of grieving (or not), this friend was gungho about getting on dating apps, going on dates, hooking up, and meeting new people. They're feeling free and optimistic about dating—the world is their oyster! Now think about the friend who's been single for a little longer, maybe two or more years. That person might not have the same energetic, optimistic outlook on dating; they might not even be dating at all.

This is a normal pattern that we see all the time in our groups of friends and is a pattern that is supported by the research.

Those who have been single for *longer than a year* are more likely to *hate or dislike* the dating process (41%), while those who have been single for *less than a year* are much more optimistic (only 29% say they *hate or dislike* the dating process). Those who have been single for longer than a year are also much less likely to be going on dates compared to those who have been single for less than a year. Of those who have been single for longer than a year, 60% say they don't go on *any* dates in a typical month, compared to only 26% of people who have been single for less than a year.

The bottom line is this: Newly single people are way more active in the dating world. Understandably, people who have been single for less than a year tend to enjoy some of the things that they've missed about being single. They are more likely to say they enjoy feeling desirable or attractive, being pursued by people who are interested in them, or hooking up with people. These are all things that are less of a novelty to people who have been single for longer than a year.

It might be easier for newly single people to feel optimistic about dating. If you've been single for longer than a year, you might be a little more cynical and a little less eager to get back out there. Let's look at how attitudes can differ between these two groups of people. If you've been single for *longer than a year*, you are significantly more likely to agree with these statements compared to those who have been single for *less than a year*.

- I assume other people go on way more dates than I do (70% vs. 51%)
- I don't know where to meet single people in real life (52% vs. 31%)
- I feel a little hopeless about my dating life (50% vs. 38%)
- I struggle with low self-esteem and lack of confidence in myself (49% vs. 28%)

Overall, people who have been single for longer than a year seem to feel a little more discouraged than the newly single.

They are more likely to struggle with low self-esteem and feeling optimistic about dating. While it may be frustrating to feel like you are perpetually single, remember that you are in good company. A whopping 76% of single people have been single for *longer than a year* (17% of whom have never been in a relationship). If you are in this group of people who constitute the majority of single people, take a minute to reflect on your own attitudes about dating.

Tough Love

If you have been single for longer than a year, do some self-reflection. Are you feeling pessimistic about dating? Are there any negative thoughts that you can actively try to prove wrong? Now is the time to try to reinvigorate yourself. Try to reframe attitudes like "I find it difficult to date in my city." You likely haven't exhausted every option of where to meet people in your city. You might not have even tried to meet people recently! Consider reframing some of your old thought patterns about dating.

5

Why Is No One Approaching Me?

This is something that I've talked about endlessly with friends, family, and strangers around Los Angeles: Why aren't people approaching each other? And how can we change this?

I would venture to say that I'm out and about pretty often (despite my dad's assumption that I never leave my apartment). I am active during the day, going to the gym, coffee shop, beach volleyball, dog park, grocery store, brunch, hanging out with friends, etc. I don't go out very often at night, but when I do, it's usually to a restaurant or mellow bar with friends. Despite being out quite often, I am almost never approached by people trying to initiate a conversation with me. I used to take it personally that no one was approaching me and wondered what I was doing wrong.

When I started talking about this more and more with friends, it became clear that a lot of them felt the same way—no one is approaching them. I included a question about this in the survey to see if what we're all observing is actually true, and when I saw the data, I breathed a sigh of relief—it wasn't just me.

As you can see on the next page, a whopping 89% of single people say they are *never, rarely*, or *sometimes* approached by people who express some degree of romantic interest in them. That means that despite your best outfit, your bangin' hairdo, and your A+ wing (wo)man, the chances are high that you will still come home from the bar without one person approaching you to make conversation.

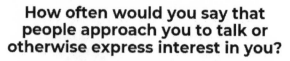

How often would you say that people approach you to talk or otherwise express interest in you?

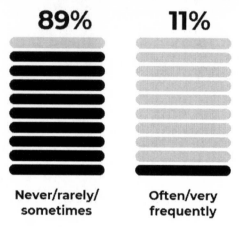

89%	11%
Never/rarely/ sometimes	Often/very frequently

Kinda depressing, right? But I didn't need to tell you that because you've all experienced it. This data should serve as a way to validate your feelings because, again, it's not just you. In fact, the vast majority of *both* genders report that they're rarely approached. You might be wondering if there is anything you can do to increase your chances of someone initiating a conversation with you. Indeed, many variables impact whether or not this happens; some of them are in your control and others are very much not in your control. We'll take a look at both kinds of variables so you can poise yourself as optimally as possible to be approached by others.

The first thing that you might think is impacting whether people approach you is your physical attractiveness. By only using self-reported survey data, it is impossible to get an objective rating of this. There's also no such thing as an "objective" rating of physical attractiveness because it is not a universal thing:

Everyone has different preferences for who they find attractive. The closest you could get to measuring attractiveness is to simply ask people how confident they are in their own physical appearance on a scale of 1-10, where 1 is "not at all confident," and 10 is "very confident." Here's the spread:

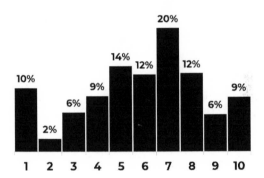

On a scale of 1-10, how confident are you in your own appearance and physical attractiveness?

Almost half of single people rate their confidence as a 7 or higher—nice! Now, why is this important? It's important because this is a *self-rating*. It has everything to do with how *you* perceive yourself and nothing to do with how *others* perceive you. We all know beautiful people who think they are ugly and ugly people who think they are beautiful. If you rate yourself as a 7 or higher, you are probably pretty confident in the way you look, while those who rate themselves a 6 or lower are less confident.

Let's get back to the topic of being approached. It's not necessarily your *actual* level of attractiveness that impacts your likelihood of being approached, but it's your *confidence* in how attractive you are. Of the people who say they are approached *often* or *very frequently*, 83% rated their confidence in their appearance as a 7 or higher, and only 17% rated their confidence as a 6 or lower. It's clear that the people who are most confident in the way they look are the most likely to be approached.

So when it comes to being approached, the first variable in your control is your confidence in the way you look. The more confident you are in yourself, the more likely people are to approach you. I do think confidence and life satisfaction are highly correlated; it's hard to have one without the other. For those of you who struggle with your confidence, I completely understand that changing this is *much* easier said than done. It takes a lot of time, energy, and determination to undo years of low self-esteem. I've struggled with these things for years, and it's only through an embarrassing amount of self-help books, countless hours of therapy, and constant reflection that I've learned to develop a baseline level of confidence.

You'll have to experiment in order to find the best way to develop more confidence and happiness because it can be drastically different for everyone. It's going to be a process of trial and error. Some things that help me build confidence and happiness may do nothing for you and vice versa. For example, positive affirmations have done absolutely nothing for me, but other people swear that their lives have changed by repeating the same positive affirmations every morning. Remember, developing confidence isn't about changing your *actual* appearance; it's just about changing how confident you are in yourself and your appearance. Below is a list of a few things I've tried to enhance my happiness and confidence. If you're looking for a confidence boost, pick one or two of these things to implement and try to stick with them for a month. At the end of the month, reassess if the things you implemented have made any difference in the way you feel about yourself and your life. You may have to try a few before you find the right combination of things that help you live your best life.

Start exercising (optimally in the morning, but anytime will do). I'm a *huge* advocate for exercising, but not for the same reasons as most other people. A lot of people exercise to lose weight and improve their physical appearance. I personally don't think this is strong enough motivation because, if you don't see physical changes, it's easy to get discouraged and give up. This is why it's important to reframe the reason you should exercise: for the numerous mental health benefits that come with it. Exercising is basically a miracle drug—it has been scientifically proven to improve mood, boost energy, reduce stress, and improve self-confidence. And if you can manage to exercise in the morning (one of my favorite things to preach about), you start your day with a rush of feel-good endorphins, which can completely change the way you carry yourself throughout the day. There are infinite types of exercise, so get creative and find the type that works for you. Find something that you enjoy and that gives you the most confidence in yourself. For some people, that might mean lifting weights (feeling powerful and strong) and for others that might mean taking a Zumba class (feeling sexy and free). Exercising should not be a chore; it should be something that you look forward to because it makes you feel amazing.

Spend a few extra minutes getting ready in the morning. It's crazy what a little investment in your outward appearance can do for your confidence. Try taking an extra ten minutes in the morning to put on a nice outfit, style your hair, spritz yourself with cologne or perfume, put on makeup, etc. Notice if you carry yourself any differently on these days. Ladies, lipstick was a game changer for me (but I had to go through a few brands before I found one that didn't end up on my teeth). An awesome stay-all-day lipstick has me strutting around the office like the boss lady I want to be. To take the guess work out of it for you, my tried-and-true favorite is Stay All Day Liquid Lipstick by Stila.

Amp up your wardrobe. Having a personal sense of style can give you more confidence in the way you carry yourself. For many people, it's easy to blow off your wardrobe and style. Trust me—I've blown it off my whole life. Since I graduated from college, I've had a consistent workplace uniform of leggings, an oversized sweater, and boots, which means I've basically looked like a potato sack since 2013. But over the last couple of years, I've started using an affordable personal styling/shopping service called Trunk Club to slowly add nicer clothes to my wardrobe. Because I have no fashion sense, I was set up with a stylist who ships me a personalized box of trendy clothing, shoes, etc. each month for me to try on and purchase. These kinds of styling services are available for both men and women and are incredibly affordable (usually $25 a month for a stylist fee). Trust me when I say that investing a little time and money into your wardrobe goes a long way in developing your confidence (I'm looking at you, too, fellas).

Find something to be passionate about outside of your day job. Having a hobby or passion outside of work can give you fulfillment, joy, and confidence that you just can't get from your day job. Only 55% of single people report having hobbies or activities that they participate in outside of their main job. Having a hobby helps build your self-confidence because it gives you a sense of pride and accomplishment. Of those people with hobbies, 57% report that they are satisfied with life overall, while only 43% of people who don't have hobbies report high overall life satisfaction. Your hobby can be anything that brings you joy, and don't worry about whether you're *actually* good at it. For a while, I didn't want to tell people my hobby was watercoloring because I was phenomenally bad at it, but it brought me a sense of peace and happiness. It didn't matter how bad my paintings were—I loved it! Don't be discouraged if you aren't the Picasso of your hobby. Just do it because it makes you happy and gives you a sense of accomplishment. As a bonus, you'll also feel a little flutter of pride everytime you tell someone about your hobby and they say, "Wow, that's awesome. I wish I had a hobby."

Talk to a therapist. I love therapy and could talk about its benefits all day. I like to talk openly about going to therapy because it's important to break down the negative stigma that is sometimes associated with it. Feeling ashamed or judged for going to therapy can prevent a lot of people from seeking help, and that's not cool. No issue is too big or too small for therapy. In fact, I think everyone could benefit from a weekly session because it's that profoundly impactful to take an hour out of your week for self-reflection. Working on yourself and your happiness is sexy, and no one should ever feel embarrassed about seeking out therapy. In the very beginning of the book, we saw that only 28% of single people say they talk openly with people about how their dating successes and failures make them feel. A therapist is the perfect person to talk to about these wins and losses! Unfortunately, mental health coverage and benefits are still nowhere near as good as they should be, and seeing a therapist can still be very cost-prohibitive. If you have the means to go to a therapist, he or she can be instrumental in helping you to develop the self-confidence and self-esteem you might have lost or suppressed over the years. Therapists help you to question that little voice in the back of your head that says you aren't good enough. Try contacting your insurance company to find out if they have any coverage for mental health benefits. If not, you can look for sliding scale therapists in your area that might flex to what you can afford. Other affordable options are tech-based apps and websites, such as Joyable and Talkspace.

Make your bed every morning. My mom always stressed the importance of making my bed every morning. I used to hate it because I just didn't get it. Why make the bed if I'm just going to get back in it tonight? According to the survey, 64% of single people are on Team Don't-Make-The-Bed-Everyday, but I'm here to tell you that mom knows best (how have we not learned this by now?). There have been several studies that show that people who make their beds every morning report higher levels of happiness and life satisfaction than those who don't make their beds. People who make their bed every morning are also more likely to enjoy their jobs, own a home, and exercise frequently compared to people who don't make their bed. There's something about starting your morning with a small accomplishment and coming home to a tidy environment that does wonders for your mental state. There is nothing to lose and apparently everything to gain with this small act. After all, it takes less than ninety seconds (please note that times will vary depending on the intricacies of your throw pillow arrangement). So go forth, make your mom proud, and make that bed every morning!

Make an effort to be social. Every day, make an effort to call, text, or visit someone you love, whether it's your best friend, mom, or someone you haven't seen in a long time. Even sending a brief message that says, "Thinking about you!" can boost your mood. Reminding yourself that you have loved ones and a support system can give you an inherent sense of confidence and happiness. In the modern world, it's easy to start feeling isolated if we haven't seen or spoken to friends in a few days or weeks. You might even be testing your friends to see if they love you enough to reach out to you first. Cut that shit out. If you've been waiting for someone to text you first, swallow your pride and text them. Get in the habit of reaching out to people when they cross your mind. I promise that they will be happy to hear from you. For extra funsies, try calling people instead of texting them—I've found that calling has more of an immediate mood-boosting effect than texting.

Read some self-help books. There are a ton of books on ways to find happiness, joy, and confidence. I've read a lot of them, and I haven't even scratched the surface. Self-help books can be profoundly helpful if you find the right one that resonates with you. I could spend the rest of the book talking about how important it is to love yourself, but instead, I will point you to an expert on the topic: Kristin Neff, who is the leading researcher on the benefits of self-compassion and self-love. Her book *Self-*

Compassion: The Proven Power of Being Kind to Yourself was both eye-opening and life-changing for me, and I recommended it every chance I get.

I'll say it one more time for the people in the back: Confidence is the number one thing in your control to increase your chances of people approaching you. Confidence is sexy. You know it and I know it, so let's get to work on it.

The second variable in your control is who you are with when you are hoping to be approached by someone. Take a second to think about who you spend time with when you're out in public. Think about the times you go out to a bar, club, restaurant, coffee shop, etc. Who are you normally with? How many people? What gender are they?

When are you <u>most</u> likely to approach someone?

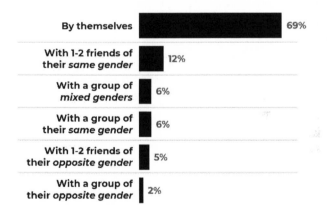

By themselves	69%
With 1-2 friends of their *same gender*	12%
With a group of *mixed genders*	6%
With a group of their *same gender*	6%
With 1-2 friends of their *opposite gender*	5%
With a group of their *opposite gender*	2%

It may seem trivial, but both who and how many people you are with play a huge role in how likely someone is to approach you. Of the single people surveyed, 69% say they are *most likely* to approach someone when they are **by themselves**. This seems intuitive; it's much easier to approach someone and start a conversation when you don't have other people watching or judging you.

The next best time to approach someone is when they are with *one or two friends of the same gender*, but even that is a distant second to the likelihood of approaching someone when they are by themselves. Knowing this little nugget is crucial to how we go about our daily lives. A lot of people don't enjoy going places alone. Most of the time, it's more fun to have a friend around because you never have to feel bored, alone, or vulnerable. But, remember, getting out of our comfort zone is the name of the game.

How often do you go somewhere alone with the same determination to meet someone as when you went somewhere with a group of people? Meaning that you've put on a great outfit, tidied yourself up, and left the house single and ready to mingle—all by yourself. I'm guessing it doesn't happen often. Doing so feels unnatural, especially if you're used to being surrounded by friends. Since beginning this research, I've started putting on a nice outfit, tidying myself up, and going to a coffee shop, mall, or grocery store—alone. Not only does being alone make me more approachable to people who might be interested in me, but it also makes me way more likely to start a conversation with someone since I don't have the safety blanket of having a friend with me. I also have the confidence of looking nice and putting my best foot forward, especially compared to when I leave the house in workout clothes praying that I don't run into anyone.

Tough Love

Try to go to more places alone with the intention of meeting people and striking up a conversation. This can mean going to a coffee shop or restaurant alone, or just running errands alone. Get ready the same way you would get ready if you were going out with a group of friends. That means no workout clothes (lookin' at you, ladies). Put on a nice outfit, do your hair, put on makeup, etc., and then get out there—all by yourself.

While you're out, be open to starting conversations with the people around you. I bet you can guess the last little bit of *Tough Love*. No phone. Being out and about by yourself is the perfect time to meet someone, so don't resort to your phone as a safety blanket when you feel alone, awkward, or bored. I know it can be tempting to scroll through Instagram so you look like you have something to do. Instead of using your phone, use this as an opportunity to practice skills like making conversation, making eye contact, and smiling at people.

***

Again, a lot of the advice in this book is much easier said than done. It's natural for humans to want to go places in groups; there is safety in numbers. Groups can also be more fun, and you may think that being in a group signals how popular and social you are. But take it from the data—68% of single people agreed that they wouldn't approach someone at all if they are in a large group. A large group doesn't sound like such a good idea if your goal is to meet people when you're out.

In many scenarios, it doesn't make a ton of sense to go somewhere alone, and I'm not suggesting that you go to bars or clubs alone. Going to a bar alone on a Friday night to read a book is something I've only ever seen in the movies, and, even then, it's not believable. When you go out at night, it's common to be with one or more friends. So what is your best bet when you're out with friends?

Well, with your newfound knowledge about when people are most likely to approach you, you should look for a few opportunities to be alone while you're out with friends. For women, it can be a habit to Lyft to the bar together, go to the bathroom together, get drinks together, go *literally everywhere* together. Again, it's a comfort and safety thing to have someone by your side all night, but it's time we try to step out of our comfort zones.

Tough Love

When going out with a group of friends, make a conscious effort to be alone at a few points throughout the night (within reason—please don't go walking down a dark alley alone). Try to separate from your friend(s) for a few minutes here or there when it's safe to do so. That might mean getting to the bar a few minutes before them, taking a couple of trips to the bathroom alone, or going to the bar solo to get another drink.

When you do go to the bathroom or bar by yourself, resist the urge to look down or avoid all eye contact with other humans. Don't get out your phone while you're waiting, desperately looking for something to distract you. It will probably be uncomfortable to be alone, but the more you do it, the easier it will get. Try to look pleasant and be confident in your alone-ness, striking up conversations with people if and when it feels natural.

Both men and women are *least likely* to approach someone when they're with a group of friends of *mixed genders* or their *opposite gender*. Let's visualize this with an example. If a guy I'm interested in is with a *mixed group* of men and women, it's very unlikely that I will approach him. Similarly, if a guy I'm interested in is out with a group of *all women*, it's also very unlikely that I will approach him (do I look like I want to get eaten alive?). If you must go out with a larger group, try to do it with a group of people who are your same gender to maximize the likelihood that you will be approached.

Tough Love

If you don't necessarily want to go out alone, be aware of the optimal scenarios when someone might approach you. The best option after being alone is being with one or two friends of the same gender. So grab one of your buddies and get out there. If you must go out with a group, try to choose the optimal group composition—a group of people of your same gender. Your last resort (assuming this is a night when you want to meet someone) should be going out with a group of mixed genders or a group of people of your opposite gender.

These are just a couple of the variables that are in your control when it comes to people approaching you. You can only control yourself and do the best you can to optimize your situation. However, you have no control over other people—the mood they are in, whether they are interested in you, whether they are too intimidated to approach you, etc. We can only focus on the things that we have control over.

However, there is one more *huge* variable that we've all forgotten is in our control: **We can be the ones who make the first move.**

6

Who Makes The First Move?

One of the biggest variables in our control regarding meeting new people is our ability to approach and initiate a conversation with people we are interested in. The research says that 58% of single people would rather have someone else make the first move (69% of women and 47% of men). When people ask me about the main finding from my research, this is it: We all appear to be waiting around for someone else to make the first move. We're going to work on changing that, but, first, let's look at some data. How often do people think they are the ones making the first move?

How often do you make "the first move"?

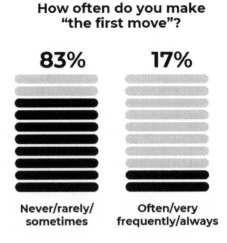

83%	17%
Never/rarely/ sometimes	Often/very frequently/always

Yikes. Eight out of ten single people say that they *never, rarely, or sometimes* make the first move. These habits differ a bit by gender: The vast majority of women (91%) feel that they *never, rarely, or sometimes* make the first move, compared to 75% of men who say the same thing. This means that men are slightly more likely to feel that they make the first move, which is probably rooted in the outdated notion that the man should be the one "making the move."

When we're psyching ourselves up to approach someone, there are a lot of thoughts going through our minds. We might be planning our opening line or weighing the pros and cons of starting a conversation. So what has the biggest impact on whether or not we actually go for it?

What plays the biggest role in you deciding to approach someone new?

	Women	Men
Interest the person displayed in me	55%	49%
How friendly the person appears	54%	52%
What mood you're in	52%	49%
How much we have in common	38%	32%
How attractive you're feeling	36%	21%
How attractive the person is	33%	47%
How many drinks you've had	26%	16%
How much fun the person is having	16%	22%

For both men and women, there are a few key factors taken into consideration before making the first move: How much interest the person has displayed in them, how friendly the person appears to be, and what mood they're in. Women are more likely than men to take into consideration how attractive *they* are feeling, and men are more likely than women to take into consideration how attractive *the other person* is.

Let's take a minute to acknowledge that the top two factors considered when someone is thinking about starting a conversation with you are two things that are 100% in your control: Whether you have displayed some level of interest in them and whether you seem friendly. We obviously can't control factors like what mood the person is in or how attractive they find us, so let's focus instead on the things we *can* control to improve our chances of someone approaching us.

Tough Love

How friendly you look and how much interest you've displayed in someone have a lot to do with whether they approach you. When out and about, try to exude a friendly demeanor. Don't be afraid to make eye contact and flash a smile to the person you're interested in. Giving someone an indication that you're interested may be the thing that gives them the push to come talk to you.

Attractiveness does play a role in how likely someone is to approach you, but it's not as clear-cut as you might think. The survey asked single people how likely they were to start a conversation with someone in three different scenarios: if the person was a *nine* on their personal level of attractiveness, a *six*, and a *three*. Of the three scenarios, the person who is a *six* on their personal scale of attractiveness is who they were *most likely* to start a conversation with—much more likely than the person who is a *nine*. This means that it's not necessarily the most attractive person in the room who is being approached. In fact, being the most attractive person in the room could actually be a disadvantage because others might be too intimidated to approach them. The person who is a *three* on the scale of attractiveness was the least likely to be approached. With this knowledge, we can conclude that the "average" looking person (the *six*) has the highest likelihood of being approached. This is great news for all the average-looking folks like myself.

Those are some of the factors that contribute to whether we decide to approach someone, but even if all of those things are present, there are still a ton of mental roadblocks that might prevent us from approaching someone. When asked what prevents them from approaching people, single people are most likely to say they are introverted/shy, they don't know if the person is single, they are scared of being rejected, and they get anxious talking to new people.

What are the biggest things preventing you from approaching someone you're interested in?

	Total	Rate confidence 6 or less	Rate confidence 7 or higher	Looking for serious	Looking for casual
I'm introverted or shy	50%	60%	39%	55%	47%
Not sure if they are single	45%	44%	46%	45%	42%
Scared of being rejected	40%	49%	30%	47%	23%
Anxious talking to new people	40%	49%	30%	41%	28%
Don't want to bother people	37%	44%	30%	37%	26%
Worried what they'll think of me	35%	44%	24%	40%	21%
Don't know what to say	32%	37%	27%	34%	26%
People are out of my league	29%	42%	14%	29%	16%

Let's look at some of the differences in the subgroups shown above. Many similarities exist between two subgroups in particular: the people who rate their confidence in their appearance as a *six or lower* and the people who are looking for *a serious relationship*. Compared to their respective counterparts, these two groups are much more likely to say they are scared of being rejected, worried what the other person will think of them, or think the other person is out of their league. For people who are confident in their appearance (rated themselves as a *seven or higher*), the biggest roadblock is trying to figure out whether the person they are interested in is single.

What other factors could be impacting whether we decide to approach someone? One that we haven't yet addressed certainly plays a huge role: alcohol. There's nothing like a little liquid courage to make you do things you wouldn't normally do, including approaching people you might be too scared to approach when sober.

What impact does drinking alcohol have on your likelihood to approach someone you find attractive?

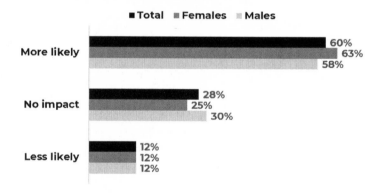

For almost two-thirds of single people (filtered to those who say they drink), alcohol makes them *more likely* to approach someone they find attractive. People like having the liquid courage to make the first move, which explains why so much of the approaching is happening at bars or parties. Women are slightly more likely than men to want some liquid courage, with 63% saying it would make them *more likely* to approach someone, compared to 58% of men. Only one out of ten single people who drink say that alcohol makes them *less likely* to approach someone they are interested in.

Tough Love

It might be hard for you to walk up to someone you're interested in and strike up a conversation when you're stone cold sober. It shouldn't be hard, but sometimes it just is. If you do drink alcohol, use the next time you're drinking as an opportunity to build up your confidence in talking to people you find attractive (with the ultimate goal of not needing alcohol to do so). The next time you're out and have had a drink or two, use that liquid courage to practice making the first move. Try making conversation with someone who catches your eye, and see how it goes.

Things I am not advocating: having a drink every time you want to talk to someone, starting to drink more often in order to meet someone, approaching someone while you are slurring your words and tripping over yourself. It would be great if we didn't have to rely on alcohol for the courage to face possible rejection, but maybe this is just our first baby step toward getting more comfortable making the first move. Alcohol is not the answer to our insecurities, but that doesn't mean we can't use the time we are drinking to practice!

Lastly, you may have wondered if the sensitive political climate of #MeToo and #TimesUp over the past few years has had any impact on the frequency of men approaching people they find attractive. Are men less likely to approach someone because of some fear of backlash or reprimand for doing so? This is certainly the picture painted by the media at times.

When I first talked to friends about putting this question in the survey, there seemed to be no consensus on what the outcome would be. Some thought that there would be absolutely no impact on men's likelihood to approach someone; after all, #MeToo is about sexual harassment, and shouldn't scare men away from making normal, friendly conversation with people they find attractive. Others thought #MeToo was at the heart of why men are not approaching people as often because it has instilled a sense of fear in them. So which one is it?

What impact has the #MeToo movement had on your likelihood to approach someone you find attractive?

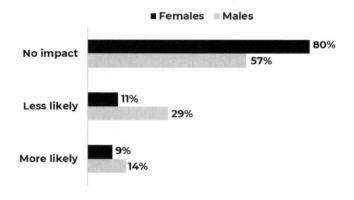

■ Females ▒ Males

No impact — 80% / 57%

Less likely — 11% / 29%

More likely — 9% / 14%

While the #MeToo movement has had virtually no impact on women's likelihood to approach someone (obviously), almost a third of men reported that they were *less likely* to approach someone as a result of the movement. For what it's worth, over half of men say that the #MeToo movement has *not impacted* their likelihood to approach someone they are interested in. That's great news because the media can sometimes paint a totally different picture of how men are reacting to these kinds of movements. Generalizing that "all men" have been scared off by the #MeToo movement is not accurate at all. In reality, it's less than a third of men who report being deterred from approaching people as a result of the movement.

7

Where The Single People At?

We've learned about people's likelihood to start a conversation with us and hopefully reflected a bit on our likelihood to approach people. But where can we even find single people out in the wild? And when we do find them, do they even want to be approached? We'll talk about both of these things throughout this chapter, but first, let's focus on where we can find them. Sometimes, it can feel difficult or downright impossible to organically meet someone in real life. In fact, only 12% of single people in the survey felt confident that they knew where to meet single people in real life, and 50% of single people say they find it difficult to date in their city.

To understand where to find single people, we simply need to understand what their habits look like and where they go. To get the lay of the land, I asked single people to describe a typical weekend in detail—where do you go during the day, at night, etc.? There are a lot of common themes in what single people do on the weekend, and a few patterns emerged among men and women.

WHERE TO FIND: SINGLE MEN

Here are a few of the verbatim responses from single men. You'll start to see a pattern after reading just a couple.

- *"Bar with friends on a Friday or Saturday night. Relax and do laundry and cleaning on Saturday, grocery shop on Sunday. Weekends tend to be open time, and if I have no plans, I kick back at home for some zen time."*
- *"Gym in the morning and casual outside activity like bowling or movies at night."*
- *"Weekends vary based on what events are taking place around town. My only consistent errand is grocery shopping on Sundays."*
- *"Going to the gym in the morning, running errands in the afternoon, going out with friends at night."*

In summary, here are the places where you are most likely to find single men on the weekend.

- Gym in the morning
- Running errands throughout the day
- At bars with friends on Friday or Saturday evening
- Grocery shopping on Sunday evening

WHERE TO FIND: SINGLE WOMEN

Women also had predictable patterns, which you can see in a few of the responses below. Surprisingly, their habits are pretty similar to the habits of single men, just with a few more workout classes and brunches sprinkled in.

- *"Exercise in the morning, run errands in the afternoon, maybe go do an activity with friends and then veg out."*
- *"I wake up and work out in a work out class, I run to get groceries and farmers markets, I watch TV and relax, and occasionally go out with friends or just a dinner."*
- *"I typically go to the gym in the morning-ish hours, run errands in the afternoon, and then make plans with friends in the evening."*

In summary, here is a list of the places you are most likely to find single women on the weekends.

- Workout class or gym in the morning

DUMP YOUR PHONE, FIND YOUR PERSON

- Brunch with friends in the late morning
- Running errands in the afternoon
- Out with friends at a restaurant or bar in the evening
- Grocery shopping or farmers' markets during the day

If you're reading these lists and thinking that these places sound fairly obvious, that's a good sign! Single people aren't that mysterious after all, and they aren't hiding away in glamorous places. In fact, they're usually around town doing totally normal things. However, only 29% of single people say they are constantly on the lookout for other single folks. It's not a matter of *encountering* single people (because they are literally everywhere), but a matter of *intentionally looking* for them. Being on the lookout for single people shouldn't consume your every waking thought, but it would be beneficial for you to be more open-minded about the places where you might meet them. Be "on the lookout" in the same types of places where you typically spend your time, whether that's a gym, coffee shop, drug store, grocery store, or restaurant. You will find more single people simply by being more aware of your surroundings.

This has given us a brief glimpse into the habits of other single people, but it's worth our time to examine our own habits as well. Your parents are right when they say you aren't going to meet someone by sitting on the couch. Mr. or Mrs. Right isn't going to kick down your apartment door. Here are two related statistics that we need to be aware of:

- 66% of single people say that, most of the time, they would rather stay home and relax than go out (and this number increases in older age groups).
- 65% of single people say that they typically go to the same places during their weekly routine (also increases in older age groups).

If you fall into either of these groups, it's possible that these two things might be a road block in your attempts to meet someone. So let's focus on two changes we need to make to our current habits: We need to get out in the world more often (even when it's tempting to just stay at home), and we need to mix up our routines so we are always exposing ourselves to new people and new places.

Let's do an exercise that will examine our daily routines. Open (or draw) a spreadsheet and create seven columns, one for each day of the week. Then, create about fifteen rows, one for each hour of the day that you are typically awake. For each day of the week, list out hour-by-hour where you typically are at that time, using last week as your guide. Try to be as detailed as possible.

Now, we're going to format some of the cells in order to visualize where you have opportunities to meet single people in real life. First, strikethrough the cells when you're at home and fill them with black. This represents where it is extremely unlikely that you will meet a single person in real life (except for burglars or repairmen who may end up in your apartment). Next, gray out the time slots when you're at work; that's a gray area (pun intended) where it's not your main priority to meet someone, but there is certainly the possibility that it could happen. Lastly, when you're out and about somewhere other than work or home, bold the text and leave those cells white; this represents the only time where it is physically possible to meet a single person in real life. When you're done, it might look something like this:

	Mon.	Tues.	Wed.	Thurs.	Fri.	Sat.	Sun.
6-7am	Walk dog	Walk dog	Walk dog	Walk dog	Walk dog	Home	Home
7-8am	Gym	Gym	Gym	Home	Gym	Home	Home
8-9am	Gym	Gym	Gym	Home	Gym	Home	Home
9-10am	Work	Work	Work	Work	Work	Gym	Gym
10-11am	Work	Work	Work	Work	Work	Brunch w/friends	Coffee shop
11-12pm	Work	Work	Work	Work	Work	Brunch w/friends	Coffee shop
12-1pm	Work	Work	Work	Work	Work	Running errands	Coffee shop
1-2pm	Work	Work	Work	Work	Work	Running errands	Coffee shop
2-3pm	Work	Work	Work	Work	Work	Running errands	Coffee shop
3-4pm	Work	Work	Work	Work	Work	Running errands	Home
4-5pm	Work	Work	Work	Work	Work	Running errands	Home
5-6pm	Work	Work	Work	Work	Work	Home	Home
6-7pm	Dinner out	Home	GRE class	Work	Home	Home	Grocery shopping
7-8pm	Dinner out	Home	GRE class	Therapy	Home	Dinner/drinks	Home
8-9pm	Home	Home	GRE class	Home	Home	Dinner/drinks	Home
9-10pm	Home	Home	Home	Home	Home	Dinner/drinks	Home
After 10pm	Home	Home	Home	Home	Home	Dinner/drinks	Home

The purpose of this exercise is twofold. First, it's showing you how much time you spend at home (black) versus how much time you spend out in the world (white). Looking at my schedule, I can see that, at least two days of the week, I go to work and then come straight home. On Sundays, I spend the majority of the day at home, aside from a stint at the coffee shop and the grocery store. The goal here is to minimize the amount of "black" in our schedules by spending less time at home. Remember, the only way to meet people in real life is to be out of the house... in real life.

Tough Love

Spend some time brainstorming ways to add more "white" to your schedule and ways to minimize the "black" in your schedule. Maximize the time you spend out in public and minimize the time you spend at home. Do this in a variety of ways, including mixing up your routines and looking for opportunities to get out of the house. Below are some motivators for getting out in the world.

Think of typical tasks you would do from home and do them elsewhere. For example, if you need to work, study, or read, get out of the house and do it somewhere with people around. Coffee shops and casual restaurants are a great place to get some work done.

Make a goal to spend a couple of nights per week out somewhere. That can mean going to a bar with a friend on Saturday night (instead of watching Netflix), going to a coffee shop on Tuesday evening to finish up work (instead of staying late at the office), or eating at Chipotle on a Thursday evening (instead of ordering it for take-out).

Take a class on something you're interested in.
There has to be something in the back of your mind
that you've always wanted to learn. Pottery? Martial
arts? Those things expand your horizons and expose
you to new groups of people. While not essential, it
would be optimal if the class you choose has a demographic that suits your relationship interests. For
example, I recently took a watercolor class at a local
junior college on Sunday afternoons. While it was
great to learn more about something I'm interested in,
the class was largely comprised of female senior citi-
zens and didn't necessarily do much to further my
goal of meeting my husband. Brainstorm some things
that you're interested in, and see if there are meetups
or classes near you that you could go to (CourseHorse
and Meetup are two great websites for this).

The second purpose of this exercise is to draw your attention to
your weekly routine. If you look at my schedule, you'll see that I
go to the same gym. Every morning. At the same time. Humans
are creatures of habits, and a steady routine gives us comfort,
but we need to look at our habits through the lens of a single
person trying to meet new people. We need to optimize the time
that we spend outside of the house by putting ourselves in the
best possible position to meet new people.

For example, if the same twenty women are in my workout
class every morning at seven, I'm not really "optimizing" the
time that I'm spending outside the house for meeting new people. Instead of going to the same class every morning, maybe I
switch up my routine once a week. I could go to the 6 a.m. class,
the 6 p.m. class, or opt for a different gym/class altogether. Most
days, I will go to the 7 a.m. class because it works well with my
schedule, but once a week, I'll mix it up and try something different.

Little changes like this will start to expose you to new people and places. Imagine if you took every aspect of your routine and switched it up just once per week. In just seven days, you would have several opportunities to meet a whole new group of people. Remember that you don't have to disrupt your entire life to make this work. You can continue going to the places you love, but just remember to switch it up occasionally.

Tough Love

This week, pick two aspects of your weekly routine that you want to switch up. Instead of going to the same place you usually go, try somewhere new. Here are some examples of easy ways that I've switched up my routine:

- On the weekends, I always go to the same coffee shop to write, so once a month, I'll go to a new one that I haven't been to before.
- The Santa Monica dog park is ten minutes farther than the park where I typically take my dog, but sometimes I drive the extra distance just to mix it up.
- The grocery store I typically go to is in a family-friendly area, so there aren't a ton of young, single people shopping there. Once a month, I'll go to a grocery store in a trendy area to do my shopping for the week.

Becoming aware of your routines and getting out the house are just the first steps you'll need to take. You'll still need to be open to starting conversations with people when you're out. It does no good to try a new coffee shop if you don't speak to anyone while you're there. Remember to do all of the things we've learned in the previous chapters about going places alone, being friendly, and being open to meeting people.

You might feel a few different emotions when you imagine starting a conversation with a stranger while out and about in these new places. You might find it daunting, awkward, scary, uncomfortable, exciting, or unfamiliar to walk up to a stranger and initiate a conversation. I totally understand because, during the time I spent doing research for this book, I would go out of my way to strike up conversations with people while out and about. It was a little uncomfortable at first, but I learned a few valuable lessons in the process.

While talking to random strangers in coffee shops, restaurants, and bars around Los Angeles, I would usually ask the same two questions after we had chatted for a bit (and after it had been established that the person was single). The first question was, "Would you be open to someone starting a conversation with you here?" I was genuinely curious if the single people who were out and about wanted to be left alone or if they would be happy to engage in a conversation. And regardless of where I met these single people—a coffee shop, bar, restaurant, or gym—the answer was a resounding, "Uh yeah, of course I'm open to someone talking to me." Provided it was a normal person starting a friendly conversation, all of the people I asked were open to it.

That felt promising, and matched up with the data from the survey (which you'll see soon). My second question, however, would cause a bit more awkwardness: "So how likely would *you* be to start a conversation with someone here?" I could see the dread on people's faces when I asked this follow-up question. Most people would giggle nervously and say, "Oh, I would probably never approach someone here." I'm guessing the responses to these two questions might resonate with you: You might be open to someone initiating a conversation with you, but you're probably not likely to be the one who starts the conversation.

What does the research have to say about this? In the survey, people were asked similar questions, so let's take a look at the places where people say they are *open to being approached* for a conversation. Then, let's compare that to the places where people say they are *likely to start a conversation*. Note that these percentages are only among people who said they go to each of these places.

Location	Open to someone approaching me here	Likely to start conversation here
Shared hobby	94%	42%
Party	90%	44%
Coffee shop	89%	32%
Dog park	86%	26%
School	85%	40%
Concert or festival	85%	32%
Bar or club	85%	38%
Around neighborhood	85%	32%
Farmer's market	83%	24%
Social media	82%	34%
Grocery store	80%	24%
Place of worship	79%	28%
Gym	76%	25%
Work	72%	26%

The vast majority of single people are *open to being approached* in most of the places they go. The places where single people are *least open* are at work, at the gym, at a place of worship, or at the grocery store—and even then, three out of four single people are still *open to being approached* in these places. Four out of five single people are *open to being approached* in the following places:

- Shared hobby
- Party
- Coffee shop
- Dog park
- School

- Concert or festival
- Bar or club
- Around the neighborhood
- Farmers' market
- Social media
- Grocery store

It's important to see this data because many of us assume that single people don't want to be approached when they are out living their lives when, in fact, that couldn't be less true. Most single people are completely open to being approached and would welcome a friendly conversation. However, remember that all of this data is among *single people only*—people in relationships may not be as open to conversation (and we have no way of knowing if the person we're going to approach is in a relationship or not).

Tough Love

This data should give you the confidence to initiate more conversations with people you see out and about. Keep this data handy in your brain for the next time you want to talk to someone and are afraid they don't want to be bothered. If you see someone you're interested in at the dog park, remember that 8 out of 10 single people at a dog park are open to you starting a conversation. In fact, I'm sure many single people go to the dog park in hopes that someone will start a conversation with them (I know I do!).

We've talked about the first question: *"How open are you to being approached when out and about?"* Now, let's talk about the second question: *"How likely are you to start a conversation with someone when out and about?"* The only places where more than a third of single people say they are *likely to start a conversation* are the following places (and keep in mind that one-third of single people is still a dismally low number):

- Shared hobby
- Party
- School
- Bar or club
- Social media

That list is a whole lot shorter than the list of places where people are open to being approached! Outside of a select few situations, single people are *extremely unlikely* to approach people to start a conversation. And when I say *extremely unlikely*, I mean that less than a third of single people say they are *likely to start a conversation* with someone they are interested in at the following places:

- Dog park
- Concert or festival
- Around the neighborhood
- Farmers' market
- Coffee shop
- Grocery store
- Place of worship
- Gym
- Work

The information from these two questions is profoundly important and is largely what provoked the writing of this book. Once I realized that most single people are open to being approached but that no one was likely to initiate the conversation, I knew that something needed to change. All of us single people are waiting around hoping that someone will talk to us, but we are not putting in any effort to be the one starting the conversation. But now that we are armed with all this knowledge, it's time to put it into practice.

Tough Love

Reflect on your own behavior when you're out and about. How likely are you to strike up a conversation with someone when you're out in public? Are there certain places where you are more or less likely to talk to someone? Start to become more aware of your tendencies when you're out of the house.

8

How Can I Put It All Into Practice?

Up until this point in the book, we've talked a lot about the issues in the modern dating world, including over-reliance on our smartphones and technology, dismally low rates of people approaching each other in real life, and general confusion about where to find single people. Now that we have all this research-based knowledge about these issues, it's time to get to work on improving our dating lives.

Something needs to change, and, by this point, I think we've realized that change needs to start with *us*. We tend to sit back and wait for someone else to put in the effort of making a move, but most of us don't put in any effort to do the same. We can either make peace with these terms and remain in dating limbo forever, or we can actively work to challenge the status quo by taking our dating lives into our own hands and making the first move.

The goal of this chapter is to shed some light on how and why people are so scared of striking up a conversation with someone they're interested in. Carefully read this chapter and take some time to reflect on your own attitudes toward approaching people. Yes, it's scary AF, but it's time for us to consider getting out of our comfort zone. Hopefully, this chapter will give you the nudge and confidence you need to do so.

Approaching people you find attractive sounds intimidating at first, so I want to give you a little nugget of information that might ease your anxiety about making a move. This nugget comes from our friends in relationships, who were asked a separate set of questions in the survey. When asked, "What was your significant other's opening line when you first met?", the vast majority of them had *absolutely* no recollection of it. They couldn't remember! This highlights an important fact: Your opening words to someone are actually quite insignificant. There's no need to overthink what you're going to say to someone because chances are high that they might not even remember it.

Even with specific instructions about what to say when you approach someone (which I'll give you at the end of the chapter), it can still be totally nerve-wracking to approach someone we're interested in. Why is it so scary? In an ideal world, we would view dating as a lighthearted, fun adventure, but that's often not the case. Making conversation and going on dates doesn't feel fun because we've made it into this big, serious thing. We put so much pressure on ourselves to say and do the "right" things when dating. We tend to take things personally, from botched first dates to getting ghosted by someone we like.

With all the pressure we put on ourselves, even starting a simple conversation with a stranger can feel difficult. It can be especially paralyzing when we want to start a conversation with someone we find attractive. Only 24% of single people say that they have no problem initiating conversation with people they find attractive. That leaves the vast majority of us who are mildly to extremely uncomfortable with it.

One of the main things that prevents us from approaching people is the sheer amount of head trash we have going on. Anxiety and fear of rejection can surge when you go to make that first move. You can start to worry about what the other person will think about you, or get anxious about how they'll respond. But here's some data that might help change your tune: Only 6%

of single people say that they think *less* of someone who approaches them. So if you initiated a conversation with one hundred single people, only six of them would think less of you for putting yourself out there. And, honestly, those six people can suck it. Anyone who thinks less of you for starting a conversation like a normal human being has serious issues of their own.

Throughout the book, we've talked about some of the negative feelings that can arise during the dating process, such as anxiety and fear of being rejected—the two most common emotions you might feel when thinking about approaching someone you're interested in. In evolution, it has been advantageous for humans to avoid things that cause them pain or misery. So if the thought of striking up a conversation or going on a date results in unwanted negative feelings, it is natural to want to avoid those things entirely.

Think about the example in school where a human comes across a lion and has three acute stress responses: fight, flight, or freeze. For this book, think about the person you're approaching as the proverbial lion. It can be intimidating and scary, but we have three choices: 1) **fight**: push through the negative feelings to start conversations and go on dates, 2) **flight**: actively run away from the dating process or avoid meeting new people, or 3) **freeze**: paralysis from taking any action at all when it comes to dating.

Fighting a real lion wouldn't be the best choice for most humans for obvious reasons. However, we *should* choose to fight the stresses of approaching people and going on dates for a couple of reasons. First, facing dating head-on will almost certainly *not* result in our death like a real lion would. Our evolutionary instincts to flight or freeze will not help us in dating because life and death are not really on the line. The second reason is that there is a huge upside to choosing to be brave and face the stresses of dating. We could meet our soulmate! We could meet friends! We need to be brave in facing this "lion" head-on if we want any chance of finding a relationship.

Tough Love

Be brave when you think about striking up a conversation with someone you like or asking someone on a date. Don't avoid opportunities, even if that feels like the easiest and safest thing to do.

If you're anything like me, you might be *really* good at imagining the worst possible outcome when considering approaching someone. You can feel the anxiety rising as you think of what might happen—the rejection, sadness, etc. Since we're already imagining the worst-case scenario, let's harness the power of that catastrophic thinking and use it to our advantage. "The Worst-Case Scenario" exercise is a great coping mechanism for when you start to feel paralyzed by anxiety or fear. Here's what you do:

- **Step 1**: Imagine the situation that is the source of your anxiety. For this chapter, that situation is approaching someone you find attractive to start a conversation.
- **Step 2**: Try to picture what the absolute *worst-case scenario* would look like. What is the absolute worst thing you can imagine happening if you approached someone you're interested in? The worst-case scenario is different for everyone because everyone is anxious about different things. Be specific, and pin down what exactly it is that you are afraid of. For this example, let's say that my worst-case scenario is that I approach a guy I'm interested in, and he says he's not interested because I'm ugly and unloveable. It almost sounds laughable when you put your worst-case scenario into words, but this is my personal nightmare. What is your worst-case scenario?
- **Step 3**: Ask yourself, "What is the likelihood that this worst-case scenario would *actually* happen?" What are the chances that the random person you approach will reject you and then swiftly identify and attack your biggest insecurities?

My guess is pretty damn unlikely. When you frame it in terms of "likelihood," it's much easier for your rational brain to logically realize just how unlikely that scenario is. It puts the unrealistic, anxious thoughts in check when your rational brain starts firing. So, how likely is it that your worst-case scenario will happen? One out of a hundred people (1%)? One out of a thousand people (.1%)? Settle on a concrete number, but whatever it is, know that the first course of action is to rationally acknowledge that the worst-case scenario that you are envisioning is indeed *very unlikely* to happen. Maybe this step will be all you need to shake off the anxiety. If not, continue to the next step.

- **Step 4:** The next step is to imagine how you would cope if the worst-case scenario *actually* happened. The first question you need to ask yourself is: *Would you survive? Would the damage be irreparable?* We know that it would certainly be painful, but you would survive. The damage done to your emotions would be temporary and wouldn't cause irreparable damage. The second question you need to ask yourself is: *What would you do to cope if the Worst-Case Scenario actually happened? What are the specific ways you would deal with it?* You could go home and cry a bit. You might feel pretty sad and down on yourself, so crying is a good option. You could call your mom, tell her what happened, and have her reassure you of how amazing and beautiful you are (my mom is a pro at this). You could call your best friend, tell her what happened, and have her rip this person a new one (or console you, depends on the friend). By breaking down the Worst-Case Scenario, you can rationally see the consequences of starting a conversation are actually not bad at all, and you would easily be able to cope if something went awry. You have friends and family who love you and would support you if you were sad.

- **Step 5**: The last step is to use all the previous steps to generate an alternative thought that is more realistic.

- **Your original thought might have looked something like this:** "I don't want to start a conversation because I don't want to be rejected and feel bad about myself."
- **Your new, alternative thought should be more realistic:** "I'm anxious to start a conversation because I don't want to feel rejected. But the chances are low that this person rejects me in a super mean and hurtful way. Even if they do, I know that I'll be okay because I have my friends and family who can make me feel better."

You've now completely dismantled your anxious thought. Maybe now it might not feel as hard to walk up to someone and start a conversation.

The Worst-Case Scenario exercise is just one tactic to cope with the anxiety that might come with initiating a conversation with someone you're interested in. The crappy thing about anxiety is that it will never go away unless you continuously put yourself in situations to challenge it and rewire your brain. If you continue to avoid the situations that cause anxious thoughts, you will never learn to cope with them, and you won't get the opportunity to disprove them. The more you practice dismantling anxious thoughts in real-life situations, the more your anxiety will start to dissipate. Maybe that's why people who go on three or more dates are significantly less likely to cite nervousness and anxiety as a dislike of dating compared to people who go on one date or less per month. They practice putting themselves in these situations more often and eventually overcome the anxiety associated with them. You must continuously put yourself in situations that allow you to challenge your anxiety and rewire your anxious thought patterns.

Since approaching someone might be anxiety-producing for many of us, the only solution for overcoming it is to start challenging ourselves more. It's probably going to be awkward the first few times you approach someone—both because you're getting out of your comfort zone *and* because people just aren't as used to being approached in real life anymore. But with practice and coping tools, initiating conversations will get easier and easier for you.

Tough Love
The next time you feel anxious about facing a social interaction or approaching someone you find attractive, try using the Worst-Case Scenario exercise to dismantle your anxious thoughts.

The last thing I want to touch on is something I find to be vitally important—not only in the dating world, but in life in general: self-worth and self-esteem. I read a book called *The Self-Esteem Workbook* by Glenn Schiraldi that completely changed my life, and I recommend it to everyone struggling with the concept of self-worth. I had never thought of self-worth and self-esteem as something that mattered—doesn't having high self-esteem just make you a vain person? The truth is that your self-esteem and self-worth have a huge impact on your mental health, happiness, and overall well-being. Brace yourself as I get onto my soapbox, but it will all tie back into dating, I promise.

One key takeaway of the book is that your self-worth needs to be *completely* independent of external factors. "External factors" can include things like your wealth, career, productivity, relationship status, physical fitness, appearance, intelligence, friendliness—the list goes on and on. It's all too common that we base our self-worth on these external factors. For example, my whole life, my self-worth and self-esteem have been completely intertwined with my external accomplishments. I got good grades, got a good job, made a good salary, and that was what I based my self-worth on. I only felt good about myself if these external factors were at a threshold that I deemed to be "acceptable": making $XX amount of money, weighing XXX pounds, having XX many friends.

The problem with basing our self-worth on external factors is that it causes our self-worth to be *extremely* volatile. Our self-worth will fluctuate wildly based on events that are completely out of our control. We might feel good about ourselves if we get positive feedback at work, but feel bad about ourselves if our coworker gets promoted before us, then feel good about matching with someone on a dating app, then feel bad about gaining a few pounds. It's an emotional roller coaster to base your self-worth on external factors.

Tying your self-worth to external factors is always a bad idea. Suppose, for example, that you determine your worth by how thin or fit you are. If you are thin and fit, you feel good about yourself and think you are worthy of love and respect. But if you gain weight or lose your physical fitness, you feel bad about yourself and doubt that someone could love you or find you attractive. In using weight or physical fitness as your barometer for worth, you would essentially be saying that Taylor Swift has more inherent worth than Martin Luther King (who probably weighed more and did less Pilates than T-Swizzle). When you use this example, you can see how futile it is to base your own or other people's worth on external factors.

Humans have unconditional and equal worth—no human life has more worth than another. Everyone's self-worth exists completely independently of external factors. Your worth is intrinsic and steady. Through all the aforementioned ups and downs (promotion, matching on dating app, gaining weight, etc.), your self-worth should not fluctuate. Self-worth is our own. Imagine it as a little ball of light that you can hold in your hands. It is a quiet, calm inner voice that assures us that no matter what happens, we are worthy of love. No one is allowed to take that little ball of light away from us. We must keep our inherent self-worth as our own, and we cannot let anyone touch it or have control over it.

What role does self-worth play in the dating world? How we apply these concepts of self-worth and self-esteem to dating are critically important for our mental well-being. In the dating process, we can encounter a whole host of issues that will try to wreak havoc on our self-esteem and self-worth. Think of the feelings of inferiority we get when we don't match with someone on a dating app, when we get ghosted by someone we went out with, or when we get rejected by someone we approach in real life. If we allow our self-worth to be based on these external factors, it's way more susceptible to plummeting into the dirt.

Through all of the ups and downs of dating, it's important to remember that your self-worth is your own, and that no one can touch it. For example, if someone says they aren't interested in going on a second date, this does not affect your worthiness of love and respect. You are obviously allowed to feel sad, disappointed, or frustrated. Rejection hurts. But you are *not* allowed to let the actions (or inactions) of someone else define how worthy you are of love and happiness.

Tough Love

Identify some of the external influences on your self-worth. Do you allow them to define your worth? External influences are everywhere, including how many people you match with on dating apps, how many people buy you a drink at the bar, getting broken up with, being ghosted, etc. While dating, constant external factors might try to wreak havoc on your self-worth. Identify the aspects of dating that you allow to impact your self-worth. Becoming more aware of these things will hopefully pull you out of a slump next time you are feeling really crappy about yourself while dating. If you are someone that struggles with self-worth, consider buying *The Self-Esteem Workbook* and reflecting further on this.

I've tried to arm you with all the information I have to help you cope with whatever anxiety or fear might arise when you're ready to put all of this into practice. To refresh your memory:

- **Don't overthink it.** Most people in relationships do not remember their significant other's opening words to them.

- **You're not alone.** Most single people (76%) find it difficult to start a conversation with someone they find attractive.

- **Go for it.** Only 6% of single people say they would think less of someone who approached them to start a conversation.

- **Choose to fight.** The fight, flight, or freeze analogy encourages us to fight the scary feelings associated with putting ourselves out there.

- **Go negative.** The Worst-Case Scenario exercise helps us combat our anxious thoughts by generating alternative realistic thoughts.

- **You are worthy.** We know our self-worth is intrinsic, and we won't let any outcome of dating define our worthiness of love and happiness.

Consider yourselves armed and ready to make the first move. You're just missing one crucial piece: What do you say? It's one thing for me to tell you to approach people more often, and it's another thing for you to actually do it. Getting vague instructions is frustrating, so I'm going to give you a few examples that you can say when you want to strike up a conversation with someone you're interested in. Maybe you only need these in the beginning, and soon enough, you'll be comfortable improvising on your own. So for all of those wondering, "What do I say when I approach someone? No, like what *exactly* do I say?"—this section is for you.

I want to take the heavy lifting out of the equation of what to say, so here are some concrete examples. Be forewarned that these may seem a little forced or awkward when read to yourself, but I made a point to try each of them out while writing this book. I promise they come off as totally normal, friendly, and effortless in real life.

Comment or compliment them on something personal.
- "Your dog is so cute! How old is he?"
- "I feel like I always see you here—we must be on the same schedule!"
- "I love your tattoo. What does it mean?"
- "You and your friends were having so much fun. I had to come say hi."

Crack a joke or say something funny.
- "On a scale of 1-10, how scared should I be about this workout class?"
- "You're brave to be wearing a USC shirt in Westwood."
- "Is it just me, or does that guy look exactly like McLovin'?"
- "I think I'm gonna explode if I don't go pet that dog."
- "I'm really trying to procrastinate [working, reading, going home] right now. Want to distract me?"
- "I'm doing this new thing where I try to talk to strangers... how am I doing?"
- "You know I'm trying to flirt with you, right?"

Ask a question about your surroundings. Seriously, just ask any question, even if you don't care about the answer.
- "Do you know any good [coffee shops, restaurants, dog parks, etc.] around here?"
- "Do you mind if I ask what you ordered? That looks amazing."
- "Do you know anything about wine? I have to bring some to a friend's birthday."
- "Have you been here before? What would you recommend?"

- "Would you mind helping me with [the door, this box, these drinks, etc.]?"
- "My friend is in town tonight. Do you know a good place to get [Mexican food, boba, etc]?"
- "Do you know where the [bathroom, cheese aisle, bar, food] is? I've been wandering around trying to find it!"

Keep it vanilla.
- "Hey, how are you?"
- "How's your day going?"
- "I'm ready for this rain to stop!"
- "What are you drinking?"
- "Can I buy you a drink?" (ladies can drop this power move, too!)
- "Have you been here before?"
- "Wanna dance with me?"

Remember that your opening lines don't *really* matter. Anything that shows that you a normal person will be a good start. Don't overthink it and just go for it! Remember that if it isn't well-received, it's not a reflection of you. The chances are high that this person may be in a relationship, gay/straight, or just not interested. Lowering your expectations for talking to someone is essential for not feeling rejected when you strike up a conversation.

Tough Love
Give some of these conversation starters a whirl. Make a goal to try at least one in the next week! It could be with someone you like at work or a stranger at a coffee shop. You got this!

9

Should I Be Using Dating Apps?

The goal of this book is to encourage you to choose human interaction over technology whenever possible, with the ultimate goal of meeting Your Person. However, we can't ignore the rise of dating apps and their prevalence in the modern dating world. Whether we like it or not, dating apps might be here to stay. People are turning to them as it becomes harder and harder to meet people organically in real life. In fact, roughly two-thirds of single people have used a dating app before; more than a third are current users, and a quarter are lapsed users.

What is your experience with online dating or dating apps?

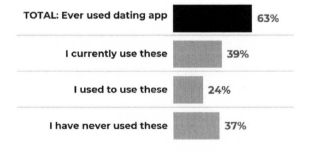

TOTAL: Ever used dating app — 63%

I currently use these — 39%

I used to use these — 24%

I have never used these — 37%

The majority of single people have given dating apps a whirl. If you are in the 37% who have never used one, I commend you for not giving in to the hype. Even as someone who didn't like the idea of dating apps, I still had an insatiable curiosity to see what they were like. There were times when I created a profile only to delete it the same day, and there were times when I created a profile and deleted it a few months later. One way or another, I always ended up deleting them.

For some single people, dating apps are the only way they know how to meet other single people. However, by relying on these apps to find love, we strengthen our over-reliance on our smartphones. We are not only using our phones to have our groceries delivered, but we want them to deliver our soulmates as well. It's no wonder that "ease of use" is the number one reason single people say they like using dating apps. But if we can't even get our grocery delivery service to pick ripe bananas for us, what makes us think a dating app could efficiently or effectively find us a soulmate?

I'm *not* criticizing people who use dating apps, but I *am* criticizing the very institution of dating apps—from the money-driven motivation behind their creation, to the detrimental impact on mental health, to the toxic dating culture that they have fostered. While there are some positive aspects to using dating apps, I believe that the negatives outweigh the positives for many single people. As it turns out, many single people agree with this notion, but more on that later.

Despite their widespread usage, let's be clear on one thing before we dive in deeper: The founders and CEOs of these dating apps did *not* create them so that you could actually find love. Dating apps were created to monetize an industry that was in desperate need of disruption. It's up to us as consumers to be weary of products like dating apps. Modern-day marketing has been optimized to capitalize on human psychology and emotion, and dating apps have their marketing down to a science. Their product is dangerously easy to market because it exploits our innate desire to find love. They show us success stories of happy couples who met on their app, giving us hope that this could be us one day. Our soulmate is out there, and every app is confident that they will be the one to connect us with them. With that kind of narrative, who wouldn't want to use their product?

And yes, we probably all know someone who has actually found love on dating apps. With 63% of the single population having used them, there are bound to be success stories. However, a significant portion of the single population has not found love using apps. Only 9% of dating app users report regularly going on two or more dates with the same person from an app. This implies that finding someone you actually want to date on a dating app is more difficult than it might seem. So if these success stories that dating apps broadcast seem too good to be true, it's because they usually are.

Dating apps are not philanthropic by any means, and they were not made to help you find love. Take a second to think through what would happen if you *actually* found love on a dating app. My guess is that you would probably delete it, right? The app would immediately lose a customer and any revenue they were previously generating from your purchases of premium offerings (such as daily matches, boosts, advanced filtering, etc.) or ad revenue associated with your usage of the app. You finding love is actually quite disastrous for their bottom line, and, if everyone found love through their app, it would swiftly put them out of business. It is in their best interest for you to stay single and keep you hooked on using their product. These apps were built with monetization in mind, and the longer you go without finding love, the more money they make. I find this concept unsettling, to say the least.

A comparison that I find to be quite compelling is comparing the motives of dating apps to the motives of the weight-loss industry. Companies that sell weight-loss plans, products, and services don't actually want you to permanently lose weight (despite enticing you with before and after photos of customers who have used their product). It would be terrible for them if you permanently lost weight because you would never need to buy their plan, product, or service again. What they really want is for you to use their product to lose weight initially. You'll inevitably gain all that weight back (and likely more), as research has shown happens to 90-95% of dieters. When you do, you'll come crawling back to the weight-loss product that "worked" for you in the past. Poof! They have magically set you up for a lifetime of cyclical dieting and have secured a return customer for life (or until you find the next weight-loss product to give your money to). The weight-loss industry is well-aware of the commonly held statistic that somewhere between 90-95% of diets fail and result in weight gain. Indeed, that statistic is what keeps their industry in business—a $72+ billion industry in the US alone.

Similarly, dating apps are designed to keep you hooked, and the creators of them want you to keep coming back for more. You may feel "successful" when you make it to a first date with someone from an app. If that date doesn't go well, you may keep coming back to that app because it's helped you "succeed" in getting dates in the past. However, there have actually been studies comparing the addictive nature of dating apps to the addictive nature of slot machines. You swipe and swipe (similar to pulling the lever of a slot machine), and get a rush of happy endorphins when the screen lights up announcing that you've matched with someone (similar to the endorphins you get when you've won money on a slot machine). It feels good, which is why the excitement of matching with someone is cited as a top like of using dating apps. That surge of endorphins and adrenaline is very fleeting, and soon you want to feel it again, so you go back to swiping (or continue playing the slot machine).

Everyone knows that slot machines and gambing are risky for both your financial and mental health, so we actively avoid putting ourselves in scenarios where it would be easy to become addicted. We do this because gambling is easy to spot and is therefore easy to avoid. Dating apps, however, are more sneaky. We don't even recognize the addictive behavior that's happening because it's happening at such a subconscious level. If you've ever burned through an hour in a swiping vortex on a dating app, you know exactly how this feels.

I'll step down from my soapbox for a minute to talk about the actual data on dating apps. That's what we're here for, after all! We've established that the vast majority of single people have used dating apps, and we've established that I *personally* don't like them, but how do dating app users feel about them?

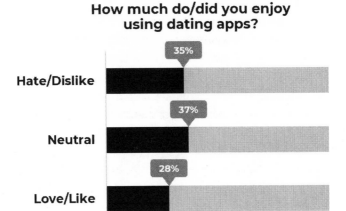

How much do/did you enjoy using dating apps?

- Hate/Dislike — 35%
- Neutral — 37%
- Love/Like — 28%

Less than a third of dating app users say they *like or love* using them. Once again, I felt a lot less alone after seeing these statistics, especially when I looked at the data by gender. 44% of women say they *hate or dislike* using dating apps, while only 28% of men say the same thing. So it wasn't just me who didn't enjoy using dating apps. It's almost half of the single women who use them!

So what's the beef with dating apps? For starters, 64% of users feel that they weren't "successful" on the apps, meaning that they didn't match, message, or go on dates with people they were interested in. Being unsuccessful on dating apps is enough to make you want to throw in the towel, but it turns out that there's a lot more behind the negative sentiment. The negative sentiment toward dating apps leads to a high degree of churn: a whopping 86% of users report having deleted their dating app or profile before, and 63% say they deleted their profile multiple times. The reasons cited for deleting the apps correspond with the reasons why people dislike using dating apps in general (note that only about one out of ten users deleted the app because they started dating someone they met on the app). So without further ado, here are the things that dating app users report disliking about the apps.

1. People can bend the truth when it comes to their identity.

It's no secret that you can alter your dating profile to show the best version of yourself—or a different version altogether. Some people take the time to construct a thoughtful profile that displays their best self, but other people can be more deceptive. They can FaceTune their photos, add a couple of inches to their height, or say they live in a more desirable city. These types of slight misrepresentations don't go unnoticed. Women seem to encounter this issue more, with 51% of them citing this as a dislike compared to only 38% of men. However you choose to doctor up your profile is up to you, but portraying an honest reflection of yourself is important.

"People on dating apps can lie about appearance and personality." – Male, 25-34

2. Two words: creepy people.

While this doesn't apply as much for men, 50% of women cite "too many creepy people" as a main dislike of using dating apps (compared to only 23% of men). Safety concerns on dating apps are almost nonexistent for men, while they can be a top concern for women. Half of the women using dating apps say they have been contacted on a dating app in a way that made them feel uncomfortable (compared to only 18% of men). Women are more likely than men to have blocked someone on a dating app, received unsolicited/inappropriate pictures, or had concerns about safety when meeting up with someone. Just check out the chart below to see the differences in dating app experiences between women and men.

Which of these have you experienced while using a dating app?

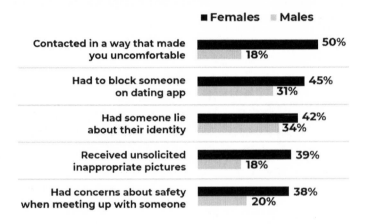

It's no wonder that women are more likely to dislike using dating apps! Dating is difficult enough without all these extra stresses involved. I dare any man to borrow a girl friends' dating app for a day and see the types of vile things they have to deal with. Receiving unsolicited dick pics and sexually-charged messages on the daily is exhausting and can make women lose hope in the type of men they can find on dating apps.

"You have to sift through so many gross messages to get to any genuine ones." – Female, 25-34

3. People who use dating apps tend to have Next Best Thing Syndrome.

The endless swiping has encouraged a perception among dating app users that there are always more people out there—better, more attractive, more interesting people than the one you are currently talking to. It's easy to allow a conversation to fizzle, especially when you know that there are hundreds of people waiting to have conversations through the app. It has made conversations and relationships seem much more disposable. At the smallest sign of incompatibility, people are more likely to jump ship, with the perception that someone more compatible is just a few swipes away. According to 35% of users, dating apps make them feel disposable and that people are looking for the next best thing.

"It's hard to have genuine connections on dating apps because it's easy to access so many people. People are always looking for what's next."
– Female, 25-34

---

4. Severe lack of honest communication and an abundance of ghosting.

Communication through dating apps is sub-par, to say the least. The person on the other side of the screen is not someone you personally know, so there is no sense of obligation to do right by this person or to communicate openly and honestly. A lot of people will opt to ghost someone instead of having an honest conversation. About 34% of users cite "getting ghosted by people I've been on dates with" as a top dislike of using dating apps. Meeting someone through a dating app lacks the same degree of accountability as meeting someone through a mutual friend. If you act like an asshole on a date and have terrible communication skills afterward, your mutual friend will likely hear about it and call you out. No such accountability exists on dating apps, which makes it an environment rife for disrespectful communication and frequent ghosting.

"I don't like how easy it is for conversations to die off and how rarely people make an effort to meet in person." – Female, 25-34

5. It's hard to convey your personality and equally hard to gauge others' personalities.

If you've ever had a phone interview for a job, you might know how it feels to think, "I'm so much more personable face to face!" As it turns out, the same is true for dating apps. A lot of people feel that it's hard to convey their personality in a brief bio and feel that they are more interesting in person. Similarly, many find it hard to get a good handle on other people's personalities by just reading their short bio.

"It's completely shallow and I don't feel like I can be authentic in a first text message, whereas in person I'm much more personable." – Male, 25-34

6. All text and no play (dates).

Playing pen-pal on dating apps has become commonplace, and 32% of users say they dislike dating apps because "conversations rarely turn into dates." In fact, only 16% of dating app users report going on first dates with matches *often or very frequently* despite 34% saying they message people *often or very frequently*. Progressing from messaging to first date actually happens a lot less frequently than we would prefer. While conversations may start energetically, they can quickly fizzle if one person or the other lags in responding. There can be long periods between responses, which makes it hard to develop a genuine connection through the app. Many conversations end up fizzling out before any mention of meeting in person. 93% of users say they've had a conversation fizzle out on dating apps, and 52% of users say that conversations end up fizzling out *very or somewhat frequently.* Texting or messaging for a few days or even a few weeks can be time-consuming, so it can feel especially frustrating when these conversations don't go anywhere.

> **"They usually don't turn into dates where we actually meet up... mostly just texting back and forth for a week."** – *Female, 25-34*

7. Apps are superficial and shallow, making it tough for average-looking people to stand out.

Snap judgements are unfortunately quite typical on dating apps, which means you will largely be judged based on your physical attractiveness. We all know that's a terrible standard, and we know that we might be missing out on some amazing people by using attractiveness as our swiping standard. We don't necessarily like how it feels to judge other people by their looks, but we *definitely* don't like how it feels when other people judge us by our looks. Those who no longer use dating apps are most likely to cite the superficial nature of dating apps as a dislike, so the icky feeling of judging and being judged is enough to drive people away from apps. Users who aren't as confident in their appearance are also much more likely to report hating or disliking dating apps. 44% of users who rate their attractiveness as a six or less report *hating or disliking* dating apps, compared with only 26% of users who rate themselves a seven or higher. It's a tough, competitive space for people who don't feel like supermodels.

"Dating apps are too heavily reliant on pictures. Nobody is interested in getting to know an average person, only very attractive ones."
– Male, 21-24

8. It's hard to discern what types of relationships people are looking for.

Because communication isn't transparent on dating apps, it can take a while before you find out what type of relationship people are interested in, which is especially frustrating for women. According to 45% of women surveyed, too many people looking for sex or casual relationships is a top dislike of dating apps (compared to only 17% of men). For users looking for a more serious relationship, it's frustrating to find people who are only interested in casual relationships or hookups. This is also a top dislike among people who have stopped using the apps, suggesting that the time and energy it can take to find someone's true motivations on a dating app is a serious pain point. People who like using dating apps are significantly more likely to cite "hooking up with people" as a primary reason for liking them compared to those who don't like using dating apps (43% vs. 17%). People who like dating apps are also more likely to say they like getting an ego boost from dating apps, and they like the strategy behind using them. Obviously, we can't draw huge generalizations, and not everyone who uses a dating app is in it for the hook-ups. However, we do need to face the fact that dating app users are more likely than the average single person to be looking for a hookup, ego boost, or casual relationship.

"I dislike dating apps mostly because people aren't serious about actually trying to date. It

seems like they're interested in the idea of dating but not actual dating." – Male, 25-34

9. Sometimes dating apps make you feel bad about yourself.

According to 25% of men, using dating apps makes them feel down about themselves, compared to 18% of women. Unless you're one of the rare unicorns who is immune to self-criticism, it can be easy to get down on yourself while using dating apps. Maybe you don't get any matches, or maybe you only match with people who you don't really find interesting or attractive. Only 33% of users say they match with people *often or very frequently*, meaning the majority of users may not be matching with people as often as they would hope. Not matching with people you find interesting is the leading cause of users deleting their dating app or profile. These apps just have a knack for kicking your self-esteem square in the gut. Unless you are mentally and emotionally resilient, it can be hard to use dating apps without taking a blow to your confidence, self-esteem, and self-compassion. This ties back to knowing your self-worth and ensuring that it's not tied up in how many matches you get or how "successful" you are on dating apps. Remember that only 36% of single people think they are successfully matching and messaging people on dating apps, so you are not alone.

"Low match rates and lower response rates make dating apps super depressing." – Male, 25-34

10. High investment—low return.

Swiping and starting conversations could be a full-time job, especially in the apps where the onus is put on the women to start the conversation. Yes, it helps women weed out unsolicited messages, but they now have to invest significantly more time to connect with matches. When you use dating apps, it can feel like you spend endless amounts of time swiping, filtering, and chatting, but often, the result is either a fizzling conversation or disappointing first date. Your investment of time and energy can start to feel like a burden when it doesn't "pay off."

"It's a lot of effort to swipe through all the people you don't like just to find the one you might like, only to find they didn't swipe you back."
– Female, 25-34

---

11. Going online shopping for a human is weird.

If you've ever found yourself mindlessly scrolling and swiping through dating profiles, you might have eerily felt like you're online shopping, perusing for a human to date, just as you would peruse for a new pair of shoes. In this kind of environment, it's easy to forget that there are real humans on the other side of the screen that you are judging, swiping, and scrolling through. You might have had the realization that if you are treating people like commodities that they are likely doing the same to you. And that's not a good feeling.

"I feel like dating apps turn human beings into a commodity. I feel like it encourages me to be unnecessarily shallow. I found myself turning down people I would likely give a chance to in real life." –
Female, 35-44

In summary, there are *a lot* of things to dislike about dating apps. For me, the negative issues I encountered when using dating apps were too profound for me to overlook. I can't justify dating apps when—for me—it usually means that I'm either compromising my mental health, investing time that I would rather put toward other things of interest, making snap judgements about people which makes me feel icky, or putting myself in situations where I might feel uncomfortable or unsafe. This certainly isn't the case for everyone! Some people may not have any negative experiences with using dating apps, or they might have better ways than I do to cope and rebound from those negative experiences. You have to decide for yourself if dating apps work for you at this point in your life, but it should be a conscious decision to use them instead of a knee-jerk reaction.

Tough Love

If you're feeling like dating apps might have a net negative impact on your life, use this time to consciously decide if you want to continue using them. If not, be bold and delete them! Take whatever steps are necessary to meet Your Person in a different way, a way that works better for you. Become less dependent on dating apps for meeting new people. Practice striking up a conversation with one new person a day, regardless of whether that person is someone you are romantically interested in. Get used to initiating a conversation with people so that eventually when you are interested in someone, you'll have the skills and confidence to strike up a conversation and ask them out.

10

But What If I Want To Use Dating Apps?

While I may personally think dating apps are awful, it would be unfair not to explore some of their positive aspects. Perhaps the most obvious benefit is that they are one of the most efficient ways to find people to date. People who use dating apps are significantly more likely to be going on dates than those who don't use dating apps. A whopping 70% of people who use dating apps report going on *one or more dates in a month*, compared to just 34% of people who don't use dating apps. Nobody is promising that those dates will be high quality, but apps are usually effective at increasing how often you go on dates. We'll explore some other things that people like about dating apps, as well. Then, it will be up to you to weigh the pros and cons to decide whether using dating apps is right for you. Without further ado, here are the things that people like about using dating apps.

1. Apps are convenient and easy to use.

Almost half of dating app users say the number one reason they like using them is because the apps are easy to use. Dating apps take a lot of the heavy lifting out of finding someone to go on a date with. This is especially true for users who have been single for less than a year; they are significantly more likely to cite this as a top reason for liking dating apps (compared to users who have been single longer than a year). For newly single users, dating apps can help them get back on their feet when they otherwise might not know where to start.

"I love dating apps because they get me out there in the dating world when I don't have time to physically be there due to work and school."
– Female, 21-24

---

2. You can filter profiles to only see the people who meet your checklist—something you can't do in real life.

The next top reason why users like dating apps is the ability to filter profiles to fit your exact preferences, which is definitely a luxury that's nonexistent in real life. In the real world, it might take several days, weeks, months, or even years to find out that someone you're dating doesn't want to have children or has an allergy to dogs. It's a huge bummer to find out things you wish you knew before getting serious with someone, especially if those things are deal-breakers for you. This a huge advantage of dating apps, which nowadays have a ton of filters. The filters you get in the unpaid versions of apps are usually basic things, such as age, height, religion, or ethnicity. You can also pay a premium to get more advanced filters, such as drinking/drug habits, preference for having children, political affiliation, and more. This ability to filter seems to be more appealing to women, 44% of whom cite it as a top reason for liking dating apps (compared to just 27% of men).

"I like that I can filter out possible good candidates to date and they are sometimes accurate."
– Male, 25-34

---

3. Meeting people outside of your network.

Another huge advantage of dating apps is the exposure to people you wouldn't normally have met in your everyday life. According to 34% of users, this is a top reason they like dating apps. You certainly broaden your base of potential suitors by using dating apps because you aren't limited to only the people in your proximity or only the places where you typically go. You have access to people all over your city, in all different industries, and all different walks of life. For better or worse, you might have never otherwise crossed paths with many of the people on dating apps.

"I simply would not come across a fraction of the people in real life that I do on dating apps. Exposure to so many more eligible people is extremely valuable." – Male, 25-34

4. The abundance of options in one place.

Dating apps consolidate a ton of single people in one place, making it easy to check out all your options and start to form an idea of the type of person you are interested in dating. This is, according to 31% of users, a top reason they like dating apps: Apps show them a ton of options and can help them figure out what kind of person they are attracted to.

"I personally love apps because I feel like it's the easiest way to meet someone new. It gives you WAY more options than just meeting someone organically." – Female, 25-34

5. It's easier to start conversations than it is in real life.

Dating apps are a great tool for anyone who finds it difficult to approach people in real life, where you often have no idea if a person is single or if they might be interested in you. Dating apps remove some of this guesswork: Everyone you see on dating apps is single (theoretically), and if they've matched with you, it's at least a positive indicator that they might be interested. By taking out these two factors, it can be a lot easier to start a conversation, which is why 31% of users say they like dating apps. For introverts, dating apps can provide a less painful way to initiate a conversation since they are much less likely to do it in real life. However, if you are someone who relies on dating apps to start conversations, know that you are likely in this for the long haul. You will probably be forced to use them until you get out of your comfort zone and start initiating conversations with people in real life.

"It's a lot easier to start talking to people on the apps." – Male, 25-34

6. It's a fun way to pass the time and exciting when you match with someone.

The gamification of dating via dating apps is something we've talked about briefly. Because dating apps are partially modeled after slot machines, it can feel like a fun game to swipe through people and feel the rush of excitement when you find a match. It can spice up your daily life if you're feeling bored or lonely. Men and people under 35 years old are more likely to cite "fun way to pass the time" as a top reason they like dating apps compared to their respective counterparts (women and people over 35 years old).

"In the beginning, it's fun and brings some excitement to your daily life, but when you get more serious about finding someone, it gets really worrisome that you might never find anyone who suits you." – Female, 21-24

7. Some (men) like how easy it is to find people to hook up with.

One out of five men say that the ease of finding someone to hook up with is a top reason why they like using dating apps. The hookup culture of dating apps can be seen as a good or bad thing depending on who you talk to. For those looking for a casual relationship or those who just want to explore their options, dating apps offer an easy way to meet people to hook up with. But as we saw in the dislikes section, there are a lot of people who are frustrated with the number of people just looking for sex or casual relationships. Many people are looking for something more serious and have a hard time finding it on dating apps.

"I've had a lot of success hooking up, but not so much with finding a partner. " – Male, 25-34

Overall, there are fewer reasons to like dating apps, and people are less likely to select things they like than things they dislike about them. However, there are plenty of compelling arguments for why single people should use dating apps. Every once in a while, you may come across someone who says they love using dating apps. Hopefully, by exploring some of the positive aspects of dating apps, you feel more informed about whether or not you'd like to try (or continue) using them.

Tough Love

If you think you'd like to try or continue using dating apps, you should figure out a way to use them in a way that works for you, your goals, and your mental health. My first recommendation would be to limit the time you spend on them. It's easy to fall into a vortex of swiping endlessly for hours on end, and this isn't healthy or productive. When you emerge from your stupor, you might wonder where the time went. My recommendation: Be intentional about how much time you want to spend on dating apps, and set timers on your phone accordingly. For example, say you want to spend a maximum of thirty minutes a day on dating apps. When you pick up your phone to use a dating app, set a timer for ten minutes and swipe or message until your heart's content. After that, put the app and phone away until later, when you get another ten minutes. Once you've hit your thirty-minute allotment, stop for the day.

This timer is beneficial for many reasons. First, it will bring awareness to the amount of time you spend using a dating app. It feels better to be in control over how much time you spend on a dating app instead of falling victim to the addictive nature of swiping. A timer will also encourage you to be efficient—swipe, start conversations, and ask people to meet up. Don't waste time swiping endlessly and making idle conversation that fizzles out. Lastly, it will start to shift dating apps into a secondary position in your dating life. They are a good supplemental tool to have in your back pocket, but your first tool should be your ability to initiate and start conversations with people in real life.

In my ideal world, everyone who has read up to this point will have sworn off dating apps and resolved to make an effort to meet people in real life. To me, that just sounds like a more enjoyable world. But let's be real—I know some of you have probably checked your dating apps in between paragraphs of this book! I still want people who use dating apps to be successful in finding love, so I might as well show you the data that could help with this.

Taking the time to be well-informed about what people find important on dating apps may help you be more successful in using them. In the survey, dating app users were asked what the most important information in a dating profile is that helps them determine whether they match with someone. Taking attractiveness out of the equation was necessary since so much of what's important on a dating app is superficial. Below is a chart of what information is most important.

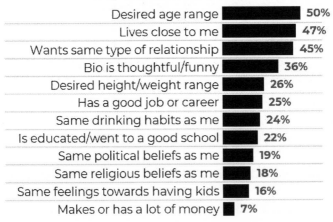

What is the most important information (aside from looks) you use from someone's dating profile to determine whether you swipe right, like, or match with someone?

Desired age range	50%
Lives close to me	47%
Wants same type of relationship	45%
Bio is thoughtful/funny	36%
Desired height/weight range	26%
Has a good job or career	25%
Same drinking habits as me	24%
Is educated/went to a good school	22%
Same political beliefs as me	19%
Same religious beliefs as me	18%
Same feelings towards having kids	16%
Makes or has a lot of money	7%

Aside from attractiveness, there are three key pieces of information on your profile that about half of dating app users take into consideration when deciding to swipe right or match with someone: age range, geographic proximity, and relationship goals. These three pieces of information are very practical, and they have nothing to do with your personality or appearance. When it comes down to it, dating app users are looking to match with someone who makes the most practical sense. Their first goal is to eliminate people who fall outside of their desired age range, geographic proximity, and relationship goals. This seems like the smartest and most efficient way to zone in on the people who check your essential boxes.

Secondary to these key pieces of practical information, a thoughtful or funny bio plays a huge role in whether people swipe right or match with you. This is one of the only pieces of information on your profile that you have full control over. You can't control your age or geographic proximity to someone, but you can control how you portray yourself in your bio.

It can be tempting to hurriedly click through the steps of setting up your profile so that you can get to swiping, but try not to rush through this process. Your profile pictures and bio are the only factors that you can control when it comes to other people deciding whether to swipe right or left on you. So make it good! Keep in mind that one of the top three things that people look for on a dating profile is what type of relationship the person is looking for. Your bio is a great place to drop a subtle hint about what type of relationship you're looking for. You don't have to make it super serious and weird. "Looking for the Jim to my Pam" is just one example of displaying humor, personality, and interests, while also making it clear that you're looking for a serious relationship. Your bio doesn't have to be perfect, but you should put more than thirty seconds of thought into it.

Tough Love

Whether you are just setting up your profile for the first time or you already have an active profile on a dating app, make sure you invest time and effort into your profile. Take some time to reflect on what exactly you want to convey and how you can portray yourself in the best possible light. There are two aspects of your profile that you need to focus on: the pictures and the written bio.

First, let's talk pictures. Ground rules: Photos should be recent (within the last three years), decent quality (no grainy or blurry photos or mirror selfies), and showing your face clearly (no sunglasses). Don't have any recent or decent quality pictures? Just ask a friend or stranger to snap a couple photos of you on your phone next time you're out! Try not to include group pictures and make sure that you have multiple photos, all of which have you in them (obviously). Under no circumstances should you deceivingly alter your appearance in your profile pictures. By photoshopping or editing your appearance, you are setting yourself up to be held to an impossible standard, and the last thing you would want is for your date to be disappointed when they see what you really look like.

After you've sorted out the photo situation, move on to writing your bio. Spend some time on it, and try to make it thoughtful, funny, or interesting. I found the best way to write a good bio was to swipe through other people's profiles and get a sense for what I liked to read on people's profiles. If you aren't very creative, Google is your best friend! Play around with your bio until you find something that works for you and gives a glimpse into your personality. Have a friend look at your bio or profile and give you feedback. While you should never lie about who you are, you should always invest time in creating a profile that shows your best self.

Men and women are similar in terms of what information they think is important on a dating profile, with a few notable exceptions. Women are twice as likely as men to say they look at someone's job or career. They are also twice as likely to look at whether they share political or religious beliefs with someone.

Some other interesting differences surface between subgroups. As people get older, they are less likely to look at things like "good career" or "thoughtful bio" and more likely to look at geographic proximity. People who are looking for a serious relationship are also less likely than people looking for a casual relationship to cite geographic proximity as an important factor. People looking for a serious relationship are more likely to say they are looking for someone with similar relationship goals and someone within their desired age range. People who have been single for longer than a year are also more likely to prioritize similar relationship goals than people who have been single for less than a year.

A BRIEF COMMENTARY ON GHOSTING

People, we have to talk about ghosting. According to Urban Dictionary, here is the definition of *ghosting*: "The act of suddenly ceasing all communication with someone the subject is dating, but no longer wishes to date. This is done in hopes that the ghostee will just 'get the hint' and leave the subject alone, as opposed to the subject simply telling them he/she is no longer interested." Even Urban Dictionary, which I don't typically use as a moral compass, alludes to how shitty it is to ghost someone. But that doesn't seem to stop people. A whopping 67% of dating app users say that they've been ghosted after a date, and 24% say this happens *often or very frequently*. Being ghosted by someone sucks, which is why 34% of dating app users say that getting ghosted is a top reason that they dislike using dating apps. Whether you've actually been on a date with someone or have been chatting with them for a while through the app, it hurts a little when someone just disappears out of nowhere.

It hurts to get ghosted, so you would think that we wouldn't want to inflict the same hurt on others. Think again! More than half (58%) of dating app users say they've been the one to ghost someone after a date. So the same people who say they hate ghosting are... also ghosting people? This is madness! A lot of people think they're "letting someone down easy" by just stopping all communication with them out of nowhere, but the lack of closure is so much more painful for the person than just being upfront with them.

Luckily, I have the solution to ghosting. It's crazy. It's groundbreaking. And I don't think you're ready for it. Here it is: *We need to stop ghosting people.* Seriously, ghosting someone is so easy that it has made us lose all sense of respect for the other person's feelings. The lack of honesty and transparent communication is one of the main reasons why people don't like the dating process. By ghosting someone, we are perpetuating the reason why everyone hates the dating process. So if we want a better experience with dating, it starts with us. Let's all make a collective commitment to stop ghosting people, here and now. I think it was Gandhi who said, "Be the change you wish to see in the world and stop ghosting people already you are a grown-ass adult."

It's hard. It never feels good to have to disappoint someone you went on a date with, even if you never plan to see or talk to them again. In hopes of easing your stress, I'll give you a few ways to let someone know you're not digging them. "Letting someone down easy" doesn't mean you should disappear from their lives without a trace. You also don't need to crush their soul with the truth that you felt absolutely no spark and aren't attracted to them. Let's find the middle ground. We are trying to be straightforward here, while also respecting the other person's feelings and giving them the closure they deserve.

Here are the best ways I've discovered to let someone down easy. They might be vague, but they are *infinitely* better than ghosting someone.

- **For the person who wants to take the easy way out:** "I'm not really looking for a serious relationship right now, but I had fun meeting you and I wish you the best!"
- **For the person who wants to politely shove someone into the friend zone:** "I had a great time last night and I'd love to hang out again as friends!"
- **For the person who hates doing this:** "I hate having to send texts like this, but I wanted to be upfront with you instead of ghosting you! I had a great time meeting you, but I didn't really feel the spark. You seem awesome and I wish you the best!"
- **For the person who wants to be blunt:** "I don't really see this working out between us. Best of luck out there!"

Tough Love

Make the decision here and now to eliminate ghosting from your dating toolbox. Treat people the way that you would want to be treated. Being honest with someone can be more difficult than simply avoiding them, but telling someone you're not interested doesn't have to be huge and dramatic. It may not have crossed your mind, but in some cases, the person might be happy that you were upfront with them because they aren't interested in you either. Regardless, people are not really accustomed to getting respectful, straightforward messages. You might be surprised to find that people will genuinely appreciate your honesty and sometimes even thank you for it. Even if they don't react positively, at least you can go to sleep at night knowing that you've been a respectful, compassionate person! You would want someone to do the same thing for you.

11

What Else Have We Learned?

WHAT HAVE WE LEARNED FROM OUR FRIENDS IN RELATIONSHIPS?

196 people in this survey reported being in a relationship, and they were asked a separate set of questions about their relationships. There was no reason to exclude them; after all, they are the people among us who have been most successful at un-singling themselves. Perhaps, for this reason, people in relationships have higher overall life satisfaction than single people (64% vs. 51%). However, it makes sense that their overall life satisfaction is inextricably linked to their relationship satisfaction. Among those who say they are satisfied with life overall, only 9% report being dissatisfied with their current relationship. Contrast that with people who are not satisfied with their lives overall, in which case, 40% report being dissatisfied with their relationship.

Surprisingly, people's satisfaction with their relationship seems to increase over time; those who have been in a relationship for less than a year are less satisfied than those who have been in one for four or more years. So how did they do it? Where did they find their significant other?

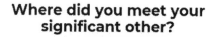

Where did you meet your significant other?

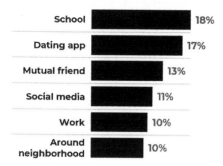

School	18%
Dating app	17%
Mutual friend	13%
Social media	11%
Work	10%
Around neighborhood	10%

School and dating apps are the two most common ways that people in relationships met their significant others, but these numbers are especially interesting when cut by age groups. Among people 21-34 years old, school is by far the most common way to meet a significant other (let's call them S.O. for short); however, for those older than 35, the numbers swing the opposite way. Almost no one age 35 or older met their S.O. in school, and a quarter of them met on a dating app. Among the older couples, other sources of meeting people become more common, such as meeting at work, places of worship, around the neighborhood, and grocery stores.

If you happen to be in school, this is great news! Take advantage of being surrounded by like-minded, geographically-close people who are your age. It won't always be this way, and trust me when I say it gets a lot more difficult to meet people after you graduate. For those of us not in school, we're shit out of luck on this one unless you do one of two things: 1) do what my mom often recommends and take up reading at the closest campus library (preferably near the medical or business school—solid advice, mom), or 2) go back to school. I've joked about going back to school solely to find someone to marry. I think I'm onto something, but I'll let you decide if $150,000 worth of grad school debt is worth finding a significant other.

Among people in a relationship, 13% met through a mutual friend, but this could have infinite meanings. They probably didn't go around begging mutual friends to set them up on blind dates, though that might account for some people. They simply met their significant other through a mutual friend; so if we want to meet someone, we should be more open to invitations from our friends. Does going to a housewarming party for your coworker sound like a drag? You may not the biggest fan of that coworker, but maybe they are *the mutual friend*, the vehicle to meeting your significant other. Be open-minded and say yes to invitations, especially ones that will expose you to new groups of people.

Meeting through work is always interesting. You have to go there every day, so you might as well make the most of it. Make a point to get to know your coworkers. It's usually a bummer when you sense that you and a coworker have some chemistry, only to find out that they have a significant other. But as my dad said, "Your mother had a boyfriend when I asked her out." Significant others may come and go, so maintain friendships with people you like who aren't single (and other people in relationships, for that matter). My only hesitation with meeting people at work is the struggle when things go sour—it's no fun having to walk by their desk to get coffee or having to avoid them at the next company all-hands.

I hoped that looking through this data on people in relationships would give me some sort of epiphany about where to look for single people. But a different aspect of the data ended up blowing me away: the reported "effort level" these people were exerting when they met their significant other.

As you'll see on the next page, a whopping 48% of people in a relationship said they were exerting *low effort* to date or meet new people when they met their significant other. If we look at just the people who met in real life, one out of two of them just stumbled across their significant other when they weren't even trying to find a relationship. However, if we look at the effort level of the people who met on dating apps, the number of people exerting *low effort* drops to 33%, meaning that 67% of them report exerting *high or medium effort* to find a relationship.

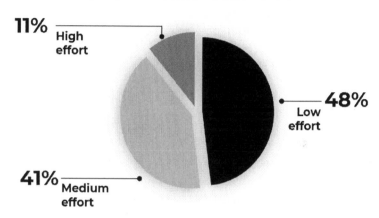

When you met your significant other, how hard were you trying to date/meet people and find a relationship?

11% High effort

48% Low effort

41% Medium effort

Woah. I'd always felt that dating apps required a ton of effort, but here was data that validated my feelings. If you're looking for a relationship, a dating app appears to be the most cumbersome way to go about it—*even* according to people who met their significant other on a dating app. So, if we take all the data we've seen in this chapter, we can draw some pretty interesting conclusions. Less than a quarter of people in a relationship found success with dating apps, so we know it's not impossible. But with 67% of those folks exerting *high or medium effort*, we can see that the road to a relationship through a dating app is a bit more grueling.

Now that we know that almost half of the couples were exerting low effort to find a relationship, what do we do with that information? I don't think it's wise to recommend complete inaction as a way to find a relationship. But we have to acknowledge that only one in ten people in relationships say that finding a relationship was their highest priority when they met their significant other.

This would suggest to me that putting yourself and your happiness first is absolutely essential before finding a relationship. Spend the time bettering yourself, doing the things you love, and going to the places you want to go. To support this notion, I will draw from the advice given by those in the survey who were in a relationship. Here's what they said when asked, "What advice would you give to single people?"

- "Love will come your way when you least expect it. Just be open-minded." – Female, 25-34
- "You need to be comfortable with the thought of spending the rest of your life alone before you can assess whether you want to spend the rest of your life with a particular person." – Male, 25-34
- "Just do you and someone will come along. The less you try, the more you'll attract." – Male, 25-34
- "Please be happy with who you are before wanting to be in a relationship! This is what attracted me to my SO, who is such a positive, fun person to be with." – Female, 21-24
- "Don't stress about finding the perfect person RIGHT NOW. I know you want to, but it'll happen when it's going to. Life doesn't always go according to a strict plan or timeline, so you gotta just go with it with a positive outlook." – Female, 25-34

In my opinion, putting *low effort* into finding a relationship should correlate with *high effort* in finding your own happiness. A low effort on both of these fronts will not find you a relationship. If you are in a situation where you are desperately trying to find a relationship, maybe redirect some of that energy toward yourself. Do something you've always wanted to do, take a class you've always wanted to take, or go somewhere you've always wanted to go. By taking care of yourself and developing your own self-love, you will develop the confidence, happiness, and energy that attracts people to you.

A lot of the advice given by people in relationships was cliché, and they were the first to admit that. But that doesn't mean it had any less merit. Sometimes we need a quick reminder, and clichés can get the job done. Here are the ten commandments from people in relationships—some cliché and some not-so-cliché.

1. Be happy with yourself first.

Instead of launching into a tirade on why self-love and self-compassion are so vitally important to a full and happy life, I'll throw a few famous quotes your way.

> **You yourself, as much as anybody in the entire universe, deserve your love and affection."**
> -Buddha

> **What lies behind us and what lies before us are tiny matters compared to what lies within us."**
> -Ralph Waldo Emerson

> **To love oneself is the beginning of a lifelong romance."**
> -Oscar Wilde

Some of the most famous writers and philosophers of all time have preached the importance of self-love. Despite all the evidence to the contrary that criticizing ourselves will somehow help us in life, we continue to be our own worst critics. Loving yourself and being happy with yourself is an absolute prerequisite to finding a relationship. You cannot fully love another person until you love yourself. Not to mention, you won't attract the right people until you are exuding the happiness that comes from within.

For further reading on this topic, I would again point you to Kristin Neff, who does research on the benefits of self-compassion and self-love. Check out her book if you think you could use some help in the "loving yourself" department: *Self-Compassion: The Proven Power of Being Kind to Yourself.*

"Love yourself before getting into a relationship. Everyone has their insecurities, but I believe you have to have a certain level of self-awareness and self-love in order to have a happy, successful relationship." – *Male, 21-24*

---

2. Get off the couch.

We know this from previous chapters, but so much of the advice we get is easier said than done. If you're anything like me, you huff and puff when someone tells you that you have to get off the couch to meet someone. I get defensive, as if someone has just told me I'm an anti-social lunatic who never sees the light of day. It's true that I'm a bit of a homebody, and I'm not crazy about going out drinking on the weekends, but I would by no means consider myself a couch potato. See, I told you I get defensive.

"Put yourself out there and try new things! Mr./Mrs. Right won't come knocking down your door as you sit on your couch." – *Female, 25-34*

We know this much already: We need to be out of the house in order to meet someone in real life. It's not an attack on your lifestyle or habits; it's simply one of those annoying clichés that we need to be reminded of from time to time. An occasional Saturday spent binge-watching a show is fine, but you do need to be getting out into the world if you want to meet someone. I refer you back to previous chapters where we talked at length about how and where you might be missing opportunities to meet people out in the world.

"Enjoy life, spend some time in communities or groups of people you enjoy. If you find the one for you, great. If not, you still enjoyed your time there, and that's what matters." – Male, 21-24

3. Put yourself out there.

There are a lot of things in our control when we are single, even though sometimes it can feel like there's nothing we can do. In reality, we just need to get used to putting ourselves out there, even if it can be difficult and uncomfortable. The only way is to start getting used to the discomfort and persevering through it.

Putting yourself out there can look like a million things. It could be going to places you wouldn't normally go, talking to people you wouldn't normally talk to, or saying yes to invitations you might typically decline. Get yourself out there talking and interacting with people. Approach people, even though you know it's putting your vulnerability on the line. The only way to grow is to continue getting out of your comfort zone, like we've already talked about.

"Get out there and put yourself in situations that might not be natural for you. That way you meet more people and eventually one of those people is going to think you are cute." – Male, 25-34

4. Stop trying so hard.

An overwhelming piece of advice from people in relationships is to just "do you" and stop trying so hard to find a relationship. This makes sense, given that 89% of people in a relationship said they were exerting *low to medium effort* when they met their S.O. They are also quick to recognize that you end up finding good things when you aren't looking for them; when you are going about your life, enjoying and loving it; when you are radiating happiness and confidence from being yourself and doing the things you love.

"Don't stress about dating so much. Take advantage of the time to get to know yourself and figure out what's important to you."
– Female, 35-44

Trying to find a relationship can become a completely encapsulating commitment, and, at times, it can feel like more of a chore than an adventure. Our friends in relationships advise us to stop trying so hard and not make it our number one priority to find someone. Make your number one priority being yourself and being happy with being yourself. When you are happy with yourself, you won't feel the need to try so hard.

"Be confident and focus on what makes you happy. Enjoy life and you never know who you will meet along the way." *– Female, 25-34*

5. Don't put so much pressure on yourself.
I remember talking to my therapist about how much emotional weight I was putting on the dating process. It took awhile for the light bulb to go on that said, "Wait, this should be fun." When we put the pressure on ourselves (or our dates) that this person might be our soulmate, it's difficult for either person to try to live up to those high expectations. Dating should be light-hearted. You are getting to know people! And if you don't like

them, no harm, no foul. You've just spent time talking to another human. We've begun to put so much pressure on ourselves to use dating as a way to find our soulmates, and that can make the entire process so much more stressful and draining. It also heightens the disappointment we feel when the person is inevitably not the one.

> **"Don't view each possible date as 'this is the ONE.'**
> **That puts too much pressure on to get it right,**
> **right away."** – *Female, 45-54*

6. Be open-minded.
I still remember reading an article many years ago called "The Case for Settling for Mr. Good Enough" and people were outraged by it. The author basically argues that settling for someone who is "good enough" and checks the essential boxes is preferable to holding out for your soulmate or the perfect fairy-tale romance.

> **"You may reconsider how high you set the bar for**
> **a possible suitor. There are some characteristics or**
> **qualities that are non-negotiables, but sometimes**
> **opposites do attract."** – *Female, 45-54*

I remember reading this article and going down a rabbit hole of all the backlash it received. Our whole lives, we are sold the fantasy of *happily ever after* and finding our soulmates. "Don't settle!" say the people in relationships. But here is someone preaching the virtues of settling for someone who is "good enough."

I find "settling" to be a harsh world for what the author is trying to say. I prefer the words from our friends in relationships—"being open-minded." At first glance, or even first date, you may not feel like this person is "your type." What the author of this article and our friends in relationships would recommend is to overlook some of the things that are inconsequential in the span of a lifetime. So he wore flip-flops to your first date. Does that say *anything* about the type of husband, father, lover, or confidant he would be? Absolutely not!

We need to resist the urge to jump to snap judgements about people during the dating process. If we stay open-minded, we might find that we are pleasantly surprised, as many folks in relationships were.

> **"Keep your mind and your heart open. You never know. I would not have chosen my husband as a possibility if I saw his profile online. He was not my 'type.' Expand your 'type.'"** – *Female, 35-44*

7. Time is out of your control.

As much as we would all love to create a detailed timeline for our lives and have things neatly unfold in the time and place we want them to, life unfortunately just doesn't work like that. Maybe your plan was to be married by 30 and have kids by 35. Life might have other plans for you. Kids might roll around by 40 instead, or they might not roll around at all.

Attempting to create and stick to an arbitrary timeline will cause you to stress and put more pressure on yourself. It can also cause you to have lapses in judgement. When you've already planned to have kids at 35, and you're still single at 34, you can make some pretty hasty decisions that you might regret later in life. Try to resist making time-dependent goals that you don't really have control over.

Though time is out of your control, there is one thing I would advocate for women who have the means to do this: freeze your eggs. I know what you're thinking. "Why on earth are you recommending this in a book on dating?" I would argue that egg freezing is actually extremely applicable to your dating life. By freezing your eggs, you are eliminating the pressure of "your biological clock ticking" (or whatever the newest lame narrative is). You are eliminating the need to find the next closest human to marry in order to start having children. Freezing your eggs can empower you to date and marry the *right* person, not just the person who comes along when the timing is right. Remember that things will unfold in time, and good things will happen when you least expect them.

"It's worth the wait to find the right person. Your ideal 'goals' for when things should happen in life don't need to happen for you to be happy and feel fulfilled." – Female, 35-44

---

8. Be nice.

An absolutely insane strategy proposed by one of our friends in a relationship: just be nice. There's a lot to be said for just going out in the world and being a friendly, nice person. When you're at the coffee shop, it's not weird to say, "Good morning!" It's not weird to smile at someone in the grocery store. It's not weird to offer to help someone carry a heavy box to their car. Being friendly and nice will go a lot further than you think.

"Being friendly and nice is not weird! Talk to people and be a good person... it's underrated!"
– Female, 25-34

---

9. Have standards.

My therapist once told me something very profound: "Don't question yourself for having standards of what you want out of a relationship." There have certainly been times where I've thought about compromising on something important to me in a relationship. I start to wonder if my standards are too high and that maybe I should consider lowering them.

My therapist and our friends in relationships are here to tell you not to do that. Don't settle for someone who is missing something critically important to you. I am *not* telling you to have absurdly high standards with no wiggle room. Sure, you may prefer that your partner has a full head of hair and makes a six figure salary, but those things should not be included in your "standards" unless they are non-negotiables in your relationship (hint: they shouldn't be).

Spend some time making a list of non-negotiables that you want in a partner and identify the top five things that will be your "standard." Things like being respectful, honest, and wanting children are things that can be considered non-negotiables. Once you've identified these things, keep them as your standard. Don't settle for someone who wants kids, but doesn't show you the respect you deserve. Feel confident in your standards, and don't make excuses for people who don't meet them.

"Don't let the desire to be in a relationship cloud your judgement. Try to be aware of red flags!"
– Female, 21-24

---

10. Don't force it.

When we're dating, it can sometimes feel like we're forcing a connection. We can easily trick ourselves into thinking things are working. We compromise and debate internally, trying to find some scenario where this could work. But the truth is, when the right thing comes along, it will feel natural and easy, not forced and difficult. Try to be aware of the times you might be forcing a relationship to work where it doesn't truly make sense. Instead of forcing things, let them arise and develop naturally.

Tough Love

Each of these "commandments" from our friends in relationships is a piece of *Tough Love* in itself. Spend some time reading and reflecting on each commandment. Which ones resonated with you? Each commandment is not necessarily an action item, but they are great reminders to come back to now and then.

AND WHAT HAVE WE LEARNED ABOUT OUR-SELVES?

There's something about taking a super detailed survey about your dating life that makes you stop and reflect. In the hours and days after taking the survey, I had person after person text me, call me, message me, or hang out with me to chat more about the survey. We shared hilarious stories about our dating experiences. We reflected on the philosophies of modern dating. We commiserated about the difficulties of dating in Los Angeles. We brainstormed and schemed about how to make things better.

A lot of single people I know cope with being single through humor, avoidance, or self-deprecation. We rarely have honest conversations with each other about how being single can make us feel vulnerable and confused. The survey felt like an opening, an opportunity to muse on the topic at hand.

So at the end of the survey, single people were asked if they had any realizations about themselves or their dating life while taking the survey. When I read the responses to this question, I was taken aback by the level of self-reflection that I saw. People had come to some profound realizations on their own after just a few minutes of reflecting on their dating life. I wanted to share some of these realizations with you.

1. We want to meet someone in real life.

The issue at the heart of this book is that many of us yearn to make in-person connections instead of feeling trapped by the modern world of dating apps. These apps have changed the landscape of the dating world for the worse. We no longer know where or how to connect with single people in real life. Even if we know that we want to meet someone in real life, we don't know the first thing about how to make that happen. We often settle for using dating apps as a last resort, but we should recognize that they aren't our only option. We can make the shift back toward meeting people in real life and dating the "old-fashioned" way.

"I just hate the dating process these days. In essence, I'd like to date in the 'old-fashioned in-real-life' way, not via apps, but apps seem to be the only way." – Female, 25-34

2. We need to get better at approaching people.

We've talked about approaching people ad nauseam, and for good reason. It's one of the top things mentioned by single people who took the survey. We all want to meet our soulmate in real life. We want dating to feel more organic, but we are terrified when it comes to approaching people in real life to start a conversation. No one wants to risk putting themselves out there and risk being hurt or rejected. Deep down, we all know we need to get better at this.

"I noticed I wouldn't mind being approached in most places. If everyone thinks that, it should be

much easier to approach someone right?" – *Male, 21-24*

Maybe, by reading how other people also feel insecure or scared, it can inspire you to: 1) attempt to approach people more often and 2) be receptive and friendly when someone does approach you. Even if it's not someone you are interested in, remind yourself of how much fear, anxiety, and insecurity that person might have had to overcome to start a conversation with you. If we can get over these fears of approaching people, we'll be much better situated to give these dating apps a run for their money by actually meeting people in real life.

"I'm reluctant to approach because I assume people don't want to be approached. While I am actually open to being approached anytime."
– *Male, 21-24*

---

3. We have to leave the house if we want to meet someone.

Do you know what's easy? Complaining about how difficult it is to meet single people in real life. Do you know what's hard? Being self-aware enough to realize that we need to put in more effort if that's what we want. I'm impressed by everyone in the survey who essentially called themselves out on this. Many people admitted that they don't try to go out to places where they might meet people in life, despite that being their ultimate goal.

You may have a routine or schedule that you love to stick to, but it's hard to meet new people when you go to the same places and do the same things everyday. We need to be more aware of the places we do (and don't) go and take steps to change that. It sounds elementary, but leaving the house is literally the only shot you have at meeting people in real life.

"I consider myself someone who really wants to meet somebody, yet I've realized I hardly leave my house and put myself in a situation to meet someone organically. Probably why I prefer dating apps." – Female, 25-34

4. We have to actually go on dates if we want to find a relationship.

Another realization that is exceedingly simple but profound in its own way: calling ourselves out for wanting a relationship, but not going on dates. Making an effort to ask people on dates and actually going on dates is a crucial part of finding a relationship.

"Although I'm interested in a relationship, I rarely go on dates and I'm not as comfortable making the first move." – Female, 25-34

5. We need some confidence.

It's hard to be confident in today's world, where social media has made it so easy for us to compare ourselves to others. We've compared ourselves so much that we lack basic self-worth and self-esteem. We don't have the confidence to approach people because we've given them the power to shatter us with their rejection. Only by developing a strong sense of self-worth can we feel confident in approaching people and feel confident in what we bring to the table when dating.

"I'm less confident approaching potential suitors than I thought I was!" – Female, 25-34

People who took the survey were very self-reflective and seemed to learn a thing or two about themselves while taking it. Hopefully, over the course of this book, you've managed to do some reflecting of your own. We've definitely taken the time to learn about the attitudes and behaviors of other single people, and hopefully reflected on our own attitudes and habits surrounding dating. It's been a fun ride together, and I thank you for joining me on it.

You don't need my *Tough Love* anymore because I think you know what you need to do.

Dump Your Phone.

Get out of the house.

Start conversations with people.

Put yourself out there.

Protect your self-worth.

Put your own happiness first.

Be confident.

Find Your Person.

Let's Talk

Thanks for reading this far! I'm hoping you've gathered some tools for your dating toolbox over the course of this book. The dating world is complicated; it's full of ups and downs, trials and errors, successes and failures. If you tried any of the strategies in this book, I would love to hear from you. I'm constantly trying to refine myself, my writing, and my view on life, so please feel free to drop me a line at dumpyourphone@gmail.com with any feedback, suggestions, or comments you may have. Regardless of whether you loved the book, hated it, have additional questions, or just want to say hi, I'd love to hear from you.

Until next time, friends.

Made in the USA
San Bernardino, CA
04 January 2020